TAKING THE L
BIKEQUIT

edited by Elly

This Edition © Microcosm Publishing, 2018

Elly Blue Publishing, an imprint of
Microcosm Publishing
2752 N Williams Ave.
Portland, OR 97227
www.microcosmpublishing.com
(503) 799-2698

ISBN 978-1-62106-090-1
This is Microcosm #260
First edition (July, 2018) 3,000 copies

Illustrations by Rhienna Renée Guedry (22, 23, 24, 26),Rebecca
Fish Ewan (86), Joe Biel (100)
Cover and design by Joe Biel

If you bought this on Amazon, I'm so sorry. You could have
gotten it cheaper and supported a small, independent publisher
at MicrocosmPublishing.com

Made in the U.S.A.

Library of Congress Cataloging-in-Publication Data
Names: Blue, Elly, editor.
Title: Bikequity : money, class, and bicycling / edited by Elly Blue.
Description: Portland, Or. : Elly Blue Publishing, [2018] | Series: Taking
 the lane ; 14
Identifiers: LCCN 2017039660 | ISBN 9781621060901 (pbk.)
Subjects: LCSH: Bicycle commuting--Social aspects--United States. |
Social
 justice--United States.
Classification: LCC HE5737 .B55 2018 | DDC 388.3/4720973--dc23
LC record available at https://lccn.loc.gov/2017039660

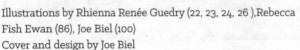

MICROCOSM · PUBLISHING

Microcosm Publishing is Portland's most diversified publishing house and distributor with a focus on the colorful, authentic, and empowering. Our books and zines have put your power in your hands since 1996, equipping readers to make positive changes in their lives and in the world around them. Microcosm emphasizes skill-building, showing hidden histories, and fostering creativity through challenging conventional publishing wisdom with books and bookettes about DIY skills, food, bicycling, gender, self-care, and social justice. What was once a distro and record label was started by Joe Biel in his bedroom and has become among the oldest independent publishing houses in Portland, OR. We are a politically moderate, centrist publisher in a world that has inched to the right for the past 80 years. More recently, Elly Blue Publishing/Taking the Lane merged with Microcosm Publishing in 2015.

Since 2010,
Taking The Lane
is a feminist
bicycle zine.
Find past issues
and contribute
to future ones at
TAKINGTHELANE.COM

TABLE OF CONTENTS

INTRODUCTION

We've been talking a lot here at the office about the difference between zines and the Internet. Conventional wisdom is that printed matter comes and goes, but the Internet is forever. I've found the opposite to be true. The Internet is beyond ephemeral—a sort of timeless dimension, where an offhand comment on an obscure forum can resurface a decade later to haunt you forever, where an entire body of work can disappear overnight, where crowds frenetically build up heroes one day, rip them to shreds the next, and forget all about them immediately. It's an exciting place of fast movement and constant stimulus. It's terrifying and I love it.

Books and zines, meanwhile, are islands of calm. They're places where you can learn to think and feel new things, trying on other people's ideas and experiences in relative safety. Where you can make mistakes and change your mind. Where you can afford to be wrong.

Without the Internet, I don't know how I would connect these books and zines with their readers. But I'm forever grateful to have the medium of print available to learn and grow in. And one of the main areas that has expanded for me, as it has for many, is covered by this volume.

I had a political awakening a decade ago, riding with Critical Mass through the streets of New York City, chased by police on motorcycles, in helicopters, and in unmarked black SUVs. It was the first time I'd viscerally understood that the government did not exist solely for my benefit and protection. That realization changed the course of my life and the content of what I cared about writing. It gave me a new certainty and a path forward.

Five years ago, the Ferguson protests and the launching of Black Lives Matter by three queer Black women onto the streets and into the popular imagination—and explosively on the Internet—opened my eyes in a new way and I began to see the scope of what I truly didn't know: The experiences of millions of people in the world, the number of ways blatant and subtle that people can systematically do wrong to each other, the depth of human experience. My realization was that I'd been, and still was, missing most of what was going on in the world around me, right in front of me. It was like learning to see a new color.

One result—I wanted to politicize this zine beyond the tacit "for and by women, or at least not sexist" definition of feminism I'd loosely been screening submissions with. Those criteria still hold, but they're not enough anymore. "Class and money" was the original prompt for submissions; it quickly became clear that a more intersectional approach was called for. Ultimately, this zine is about ways people negotiate power, and the various wedges that the powerful can use to separate us from each other.

Everything in these pages was written before the election of 2016, sometimes well before. Looking back I have a strong sense of then and now, before and after. But I think it's telling that, well, it doesn't really show on the page. The same stakes are urgent, the same stories need telling, the same questions remain unanswered. Now, it's just easier to mobilize people to care.

This volume you hold in your hands was originally going to be the second issue of the *Journal of Bicycle Feminism*, a more dignified name, I thought, that reflected growing up and moving on from the scrappier series of *Taking the Lane* zines. But the forces of politics have pulled me back to scrappy origins, and *Taking the Lane* is back, though some of the formatting intended for the *Journal* (it contains a recipe, a short story, and even a poem) remains. This is the fourteenth issue. It's been two years in the works. Thank you for picking it up. I hope it gives you some of the space you need to try on ideas and make mistakes and learn something about yourself or the world that blows your horizons wide open.

–Elly Blue, Portland, Oregon, August 4, 2017

FOREWORD: AN UNCOMFORTABLE QUESTION

Sidnee Haynes

The cover of this book features a photo of me posed standing atop a bike seat, peering over a fence. When it went public, a person who I'm sure is good intentioned asked, why is there a photo of a white person on the cover of a zine about equity and social justice?

My unfortunate initial response is: It's complicated. Or even more unfortunate: I have some serious imposter syndrome when it comes to my racial identity. While my maternal grandfather was the first American born child of a Mexican family, the rest of my origins are varying specificities of white. Culturally, there are some facets of my experience that one could define as ethnically influenced, but who am I, or anyone who doesn't live the cultural experience itself, to define what counts as white or non-white?

So it's a catch-22. It would be disingenuous for me to say that I am not a racial minority, and to some people's standard, disingenuous for me to say I am. Usually, when people ask me this in person, I first say, why are you asking? And then I say... pretty much the exact answer above.

However, I'd like challenge the questioner—and you, the reader—with another question. Can a person's exterior actually tell us anything concrete about equity, or about the theme of bikequity? Social systems, expectations, circumstances, and significant financial strain in many periods of my life have kept me from the metaphorical fence leap off the metaphorical bike seat. So yeah, I'm the one they put on the bike seat on the cover of this zine, but my story and the stories of the people inside the zine are what the purpose of this project is.

Don't judge a book by its cover, I suppose is the short answer.

SMIRK

Tamika Butler

Sometimes when I get really down, I just write. Not for anyone but me. Not to share, not to put out in the world, but to get out my feelings and emotions. I write because as a woman of color, we aren't allowed to lose it. We have to keep it together. I'm successful and doing well professionally. I'm not naïve. I know that my ability to make a joke, flash a dimple, and be laid back and chill helps. What if I wasn't into jokes, didn't smile as much, and was angry all the time?

Guess what? I am angry all the time. I just hide it. My parents taught me how. They knew I would need it to survive.

That's why I write. And honestly, I don't write that much, because if I write I let it out. If I write, I admit it. If I write, I cry. If I write, I give into the feelings. If I write, I have to stop. I have to stop working. I have to stop believing I'm okay. I have to stop pretending I cannot remember all the aggressions and instances of racism I've so neatly packed away. I have to stop being numb to the world I live in, the things that bother me, the things that scare me, the things that will one day kill me. Maybe one day sooner than I thought. Maybe one day before I get to tell my family how much I love them. Maybe one day before I finish the bag of skittles I'm eating (and the only skittles you better ever talk to me about). One day before I finish the book I'm reading. One day before I fix my car that died in the middle of the street.

My car was in a wreck today. I wasn't driving. But when I got the call, all I thought about was *thank goodness I wasn't driving*. Today could have been my day. I got the call in the middle of a meeting. I had this panic attack inside, I couldn't focus, I couldn't think, but I finished that meeting. I charmed those people. It was a success. I was freaking out, thinking *what if today was my day*. But that's what we do, push it aside, keep going.

I don't write because I feel like I don't have time. I need to make time. But how do you make time when you're constantly on borrowed time? I haven't been able to check my email today. I haven't been able to articulate to my white wife why I want to cry because I'm not sure she'll understand and I don't want to be upset if she doesn't. Another young man was shot by the police yesterday. I've had a lot of non-black friends text me today and tell me they love me. I love them, but I can't. Oppressed people will always need allies. I'm so happy that more people in my life are talking about black lives than Brad and Angie or how many Kardashians The Game slept with. I love you all. Keep fighting. But I can't today.

I keep running over and over again in my head the last time someone called me sir (spoiler alert: every damn day). Today with my baseball cap over my eyes (so no one could see the pain) and my all-black everything, I watched people watch me. I watched people wonder. I watched people try to figure out what—not who, I'm not a who to those eyes—inhabited my body.

I am pretty comfortable with who I am, but when people call me sir, it bugs the shit out of me. Today, I realized. It doesn't bug me. It scares me. I'm walking through this world and when I'm dressed and moving in ways that are the most authentic and comfortable to me, in other people's eyes I am a man or trans or both or neither. That's not how I self define, but if there is one thing we know as black people in this country, it's not how we define ourselves, it's how *they* define us.

My parents raised me to believe I'm smart. I'm talented. I'm funny. I'm honest. I'm kind. I'm caring. I'm good. I'm flawed. I'm me. I'm perfect. They also raised me to be aware that to *they*, I'm dangerous. Because that is how they define me. As black kids, we're raised to understand early that they have a definition that matters. They have a definition that wins. They have a definition that kills. Even if I'm good. Do you have to teach your kids that? Do you understand the pain of knowing you have to do it, but fearing what happens if you don't?

Who is "they?" Whether it's white teachers lying to my parents and saying they didn't offer honors classes because they defined me as not smart enough to succeed. Or when all the black students from my college went on a road trip to a conference and had a group of police officers show up when we stopped for gas to arrest us because a concerned citizen defined us as a gang that was there to rob everyone. Or white administrators not protecting me against my supervisor beating and sexually abusing me for months when I was just a college kid because they defined me as hypersexual and wanting it. Or a year later defining me as a rapist because a white girl who wanted to date me didn't like when I said no and they could still only define me as hypersexual and a predator who needed to go to prison as a result. Or when my colleague can't recognize my success as the product of hard work—they define me as cheating by using my black queerness to get ahead and oppress and threaten them. Or when a cop stops me and defines me as a suspect when I'm being the good friend taking people home or riding a bike that's too nice or driving on Stanford's campus when its only for students.

How I define myself, my friends, and our black joy, pain, hope, or sadness in those moments is insignificant to them and how they define us.

I posted a picture of me with my "hands up don't shoot" shirt. And every time I look at this picture, I think of the expression on my face. Partial smirk, partial smile, partial mean mug, partial sadness. I get the mean mug. Fuck this shit, I wish you would shoot me. I get the sadness. Fuck this. Again? Who died now? Let me get my hashtags ready. But the smirk? The smile?

I smirk and I smile because I know I'm going to be all right. I smirk and smile because I know that no matter how uncomfortable a black man on a knee makes you, Colin Kaepernick is right. I don't know if the next time someone calls me sir, and I turn around with my smirk because they don't see me, they just see they definition of me, I don't know if it's the last time. I think it's this acknowledgment that I'm going to die. And if I go, I don't want there to be fear on my face. I want the smirk. Because when they find out that I am good, they'll regret it, right? We're all good. We all have value. We're all people. Maybe it won't matter who I am. To them, I'll be whatever they defined me as before they pulled the trigger. To experience life as black people in this country. To listen to *they* define us. How can we do all that and not smirk? They don't know us. They fear us. That fear prevents them from ever knowing, ever asking, ever feeling beyond fear. Every picture, every sunrise, every sunset. It's borrowed time.

And sure, maybe I won't get shot by a cop. Maybe I'll keep eating my feelings every time I see one of my brothers or sisters get shot and that state of pre-diabetes I'm in will finally catch up with me. But tell me that ain't they fault? Tell me any of my brothers and sisters facing this ain't here because they systematically segregate us in neighborhoods without healthy food choices and options? Maybe I'll get hit by a car riding my bike. But tell me that ain't they fault. Tell me any of my brothers and sisters facing traffic tragedies ain't dying because they systematically segregate us in neighborhoods with no sidewalks or infrastructure or concern and don't ever talk to us about what we need in our neighborhoods because they're too scared or unskilled to be here. Maybe I'll die fighting the good fight (what fight is that?) in this nonprofit work I do. But tell me that ain't they fault. Tell me any of my brothers and sisters aren't out here fighting for the rights of our people, not taking care of ourselves, not making sure we're okay because they won't fight for us and if we don't got us, no one has us.

Can you tell me that? Maybe not. So you'll go onto facebook and like a picture of something that doesn't matter or that feels safe to you. You'll criticize people who don't agree with you when you say all lives or blue lives matter, but you won't do shit about any of these definitions they keep putting on us. Maybe you don't think all lives matter, but you stay silent when your friends of color are hurting and you do it because deep down you don't know what to do. I understand. I feel that. I don't know what to do either, but I just keep getting up. I keep doing things, like living as a black person in this county, that don't feel safe. I don't have a choice. You do. I just keep smirking when I see another day, telling all the folks of color that I love them and hope that when they define me tomorrow, it's not the day their definition finally catches up with me.

PEDALING BACK TO MYSELF

V.K. Henry

I ran from the house, suitcases in hand, jumped into my car, and drove to my mother's house.

He followed.

Not immediately, but within days he was stalking me at work, at home, on the phone. I could not escape his voice, which twisted my thoughts and softened my resolve to get away. The person I had loved and trusted the most in this world saw me as less than human—I didn't survive that unscathed. My relatives were frightened of the person I'd become. I was an empty husk. As much as I had wanted to simply spring back to life after leaving my husband, it didn't work that way for me. I fell into a deep depression. Pulling myself out of bed and brushing my teeth were monumental tasks. I struggled to put on an act for my family and friends, to show them that I was okay and they didn't have to worry.

After six months of this, I left California and went into hiding at my cousin's house in Portland, Oregon. I sold my beloved 1966 Ford Mustang because I had no money and no way to support myself. I had my two suitcases and little else.

I secured a part-time position in Beaverton, shelving books from 7:00 to 11:00 am, riding the bus and the light rail before the sun rose. I enjoyed my job. I didn't have to speak with my coworkers, as almost all of them wore headphones as they shelved in opposite corners of the store. I didn't have to explain myself, my divorce, or the fact that I had been technically homeless for over six months. Things were not ideal, but manageable, until it became clear that I would not able to find a second part-time job or a single full-time position. My move-out date was rapidly approaching, and I was unable to support myself on my own. I moved in with a new friend who lived across the river, which seemed to be an elegant solution until I realized she lived in a neighborhood that didn't have an early morning bus. I could not get to work.

I panicked. I would never get my shit together. It seemed pointless to keep trying. I let the malaise overtake me for perhaps an hour. I was no stranger to depression. It was familiar, comfortable. But the familiar had almost killed me and I didn't want to die.

I had come this far and was unwilling to give up. This was unusual for me. I had historically required periodic rescuing by my family and friends. But I had burned through all of their good graces and needed a solution that didn't force others to save me from myself.

There were two bike shops within walking distance of my friend's house, and I chose the slightly closer one, the Bike Commuter. There was nothing on the sales floor that I could afford. I followed the owner down a narrow set of stairs and into what had once been a bank's vault with several bikes inside. I chose a clunky silver hybrid and carried it upstairs and outside for a test ride. I pedaled around Sellwood, pretending that I could tell whether or not this was a good bike. All I knew was that it was $175 and the brakes worked. I bought it.

I traced my route on a biking map of Southeast Portland using a black Sharpie pen. I would take the Springwater Corridor, then cross the Hawthorne Bridge, then get on the MAX at SW 3rd and Morrison. I didn't know if I could make that ride alone at five in the morning, but I didn't see another solution. So I rode. Heading north in the mornings, the Willamette River was on my left and the marshy lake of Oaks Bottom Wildlife Refuge was on my right. There wasn't much in the way of lighting on the path, and I only ever saw the red flashing lights of one or two other riders as they passed me by. Sometimes the wind spat rain in my face the entire ride, forcing me to gear down as if I was riding up a hill. Occasionally I caught a glimpse of a deer foraging, but mostly it was just me, the river, and the air.

Once, I saw a beaver. My manager said it must have been a nutria.

"Its tail was *flat*," I insisted, before grabbing a cart of books to shelve.

My morning rides became meditative. Often the quiet flow of the river was the only accompaniment to my journey. Being near a body of water made me feel closer to god, even though I didn't know what that was or even if I truly believed it existed. I started praying in earnest for the first time in my life. I was afraid of the dark, the cold, and my loneliness. I prayed that I would get to work safely. I prayed for acceptance of my situation. I prayed for relief from the consuming rage I felt whenever I thought of my husband.

But prayer cannot fix a flat tire and I knew that no one would be able to help me if something happened on the trail. I returned to Bike Commuter and asked if they would teach me how to do basic bike repairs. I learned how to patch a tube, clean and lube the chain, and adjust the brakes and derailleurs. I practiced changing the tires every few weeks, just in case. I never had an accident on the Springwater Corridor, but the knowledge made me feel safe.

I hadn't felt safe in a long time. I had been broken, scared, and lost for several years. I felt that my body had betrayed me. At the end of my marriage, my body was no longer mine. I had forfeited the right to decide where I should go, what I could do, or what could be done to me. Gaining physical freedom didn't equal emotional freedom. I was uncomfortable when touched, and anxious around men. Even a friendly pat on the back from family members caused me to flinch internally. I learned grounding techniques from a therapist at the Gateway Center for Domestic Violence Services, and although that helped with acute panic attacks, it did little to sooth my general anxiety and discomfort.

Riding forced me to be present in my body, and in the world. It was uncomfortable for me, after spending so much time and energy dissociating from both. Being present meant that I could see I was becoming the woman I had always wanted to be. My body was strong; able to sustain me on moderate to challenging bike rides through inclement weather and capable of carrying me through the physical labor of my job. My spirit had survived trauma intact, or mostly intact, for here I was pedaling through the darkness, carrying on in spite of overwhelming odds. I was given a second chance. I can study it and question it for the rest of my life, or I can accept this gift and attempt to live life to the best of my ability. What I do know for certain is that contentment comes from letting go. I had to let go of the old ideas I had about myself, the ones that told me I was too weak to stand up to my abuser, and too weak to ride my bike through wintery, predawn mornings. I had to let go of trying to control what my life looked like, and what I thought my life should look like. I had to trust that things would work out the way they were meant to, which is no easy feat for someone who trusted only in anxiety, fear, and pain.

I now make enough money to purchase either a shitty car or a nice bike. I chose to trade in my poky hybrid for a sleek Norco Cityglide, because although I no longer have to depend on others for a roof over my head, the cost of gasoline, maintenance, and insurance might not be within my reach. But even if I could easily bring a car into my life permanently, I don't know that I would. Cycling offers an emotional and financial freedom that I'm not willing to trade for convenience and social status. Those brisk morning rides along the river helped me find a part of myself I'd thought was lost.

HAPPIER, EVER AFTER

Rhienna Renée Guedry

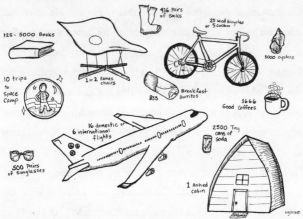

S elling my car was the literal car-for-cash swap that funded my cross-country move: 3,300 miles, a diagonal SE-to-NW, from the center of the Sunshine State to a city with a reputation as New Amsterdam. It was only 2-years old, a VW Golf I purchased new after believing I had outgrown my first car aesthetically. But this isn't a story about cars; it's a story about *life without cars*, and all the things we gain in their absence. As we enter my story, becoming car-free is the end of one era, and the beginning of another.

I grew up to both respect and fear money. I worked an after-school job in high school, saving 80% of every paycheck while living at home so that I could buy my first car.

I didn't analyze my relationship with transportation until I started traveling, visiting cities like New York, Boston, London, and even smaller cities like Austin that had a robust infrastructure for public transit. When you weren't riding transit you were outside walking. And suddenly I started paying attention to cycling, and in no time, bike infrastructure was just as important to me famous artists and landmarks in cities I visited.

Here's a well-kept secret: giving up on cars is the biggest check you can ever write to yourself. Once my brain made the shift to car-free, it was like I won the lottery.

As a driver and car-owner in the mid-90s to mid-00s, I was spending $400/month on a car note and insurance, with gas a wild card of anywhere from $1-4 depending on how far back my memory reaches and whatever weird state we were in, politically,

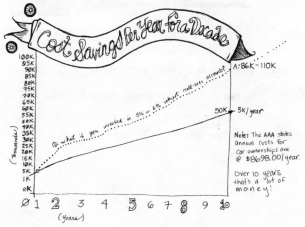

Cost Savings Per Year For a Decade

A: 86K - 110K

Q: what if you invested in 5% or 6% interest roll-over accounts?

50K 5K/year

Note: The AAA states annual costs for car ownerships are @ $8698.00/year.

Over 10 years that's a lot of money!

(thousands) — 100K, 95K, 90K, 85K, 80K, 75K, 70K, 65K, 60K, 55K, 50K, 45K, 40K, 35K, 30K, 25K, 20K, 16K, 10K, 5K, 1K, 0K

(years) — 0 1 2 3 4 5 6 7 8 9 10

with Big Oil. On average, that's 5k a year, not counting car rentals when I traveled, tickets, repairs, tolls, maintenance, products, tag renewals, parking fees or decals, and so forth.

In this narrative, the simple removal of a car and the addition of a bicycle from 2007 to current (2016) has saved me forty-five thousand dollars. Let that sink in.

5k a year.

45k.

If you won the lottery, 45k would change your life. Realistically for most working class people, even 5k would. But to save such a radical amount of money every single year blew my mind. This was my first (bike) revolution of thought.

By making a pretty simple commitment to use my legs, two wheels, and the occasional public transit or wildcard, I was self-employed: saving money, making money, whatever it needed to be. There were many times when I savored my minimal expenses, opting away from public transit to save a few bucks while my trusty steed took me as far as I felt like pedaling.

Economics 101

Here's a little anecdotal data I've observed from years interacting with coworkers and friends.

Of my friends who are car-free, most cite the financial freedom they have empowers them to buy and shop locally, splurge on frivolities, and think through

If you're reading this and love bikes, but maybe still own a car*, challenge yourself to think about when you need it and whether or not it's time to ditch the four-wheels. Is it for quarterly trips out of town? For peace of mind when it comes to transporting toddlers or pets in a pinch or an emergency? Or is it a convenience item, like how we mostly have accepted microwaves in our kitchen despite overlapping purpose in other devices or way of preparing food?

Do you have a car? A gut check:

Write down how much your car is worth Blue Book if you sold it tomorrow. Estimate one year from now what you'd have in savings without your monthly car-related expenses. Factor in buying yourself one new mid-priced bicycle and maybe $150 in random repairs (spare tubes, a new bike lock, whatever). Do you come out with money in savings?

Playing with numbers for the sake of example: five thousand dollars could be enough to fly domestically 16 times a year, or twice internationally. Five thousand dollars could be 170 cab rides, 5 customized Surly bikes, or something like 25 bicycles of the Schwinn/Nishiki/Peugeot variety, give or take, off of Craigslist.

That's the beauty of a car-free economics: riding a bike is a clean solution like you only get in math; it is perfectly surmised from the facts of life.

Why wouldn't you take the money?

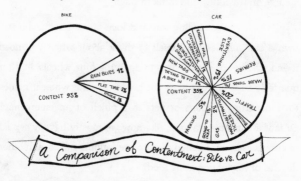

a Comparison of Contentment: Bike vs. Car

REALLY AWESOME AND POOR

Tammy Melody Gomez

I t's just about that time. I can still make it, if I hurry. Put on the layers of necessary jackets and scarves, and the helmet and lights that are mandated by the organizers and local bicycling laws.

But I probably won't go. Again. I'll stay away as I usually do, in a steady and now predictable pattern of letting go of excitement about bicycling.

Lest there be any doubt about it, I am a woman who *loves* to bicycle in her city and who, in fact, has been bicycling almost daily as an urban commuter who hasn't owned a car since about 2008. Which is saying a lot being from and residing in Texas. But I just can't get psyched anymore about joining the social rides—the Sunday night, the Wednesday night, the regularly-scheduled group excursions—as I first did long ago.

It took some time for Fort Worth to warm to the idea of urban cyclists taking up precious lane space on the public streets. Taking anything away from cars and their operators is almost a sacrilegious act in this state. But now that the wheels of time are spinning in a new and progressive direction, the group and social rides and Facebook bike group pages are sprouting up here too.

Unfortunately, the leaders and coordinators of the social rides tend to be of a specific and very limited demographic.

I'll give you one guess. They decide for all of us where we will ride, selecting routes that bypass the neighborhoods or sections of town where my mother resides in the humble but well-built home I grew up in, where my 7-year old nephew gets his pan dulce and sometimes walks to school, and where my brother waits to catch the bus to get his dialysis treatments.

Most social riders might call these parts of town "dangerous," not realizing they're talking about areas I occupy, traverse, and pedal into—often by myself. They seem to have a locked-in rejection of or a lack of curiosity about what is not known, leading to an unwillingness to go and explore where they have never been before.

What ends up happening is that the social rides are mindnumbingly predictable and there seems to be no "edge" for possible growth and new discovery. We stop at the same pubs, ride down the same well-paved, gentrified streets and 'hoods. We are racing to a destination called sameness and that is a pablum that has no taste for me. Without flavor on the ride, I am reminded that mainstreamers are comfy with what they know. Hipster brewpubs, well-lit cupcake boutiques, bougie wine bars. But that's not me. I mean, I do enjoy beer, cupcakes, and, yeah, I'll take a glass of wine—but that's not the totality of me, nor of my experience of this city.

Making the social rides about spending money along the way is another complication, particularly for those of us on a fixed-income or who live from paycheck to paycheck. It's not fun getting outed as a broke bicyclist when you're on social rides where folks are dropping twelve bucks on a cheese tray to go with their expensive artisanal pints. You kinda just want to stay home with your 40 oz.

And now for my bicycling backstory.

One late afternoon, back around 2008, I got dolled up and wrapped a gift before jumping into my slow-moving 1990s model Buick. I was a bit reluctant to drive, given that I hadn't paid my insurance premium for the month—saving that money for a greater need, I guess—but I did it anyway because of the friend whose birthday dinner was now in session. I just couldn't flake on her.

Long story short, I got pulled over and ticketed, and my instincts to stay home that evening totally finger-waved me for the rest of the week. Driving without insurance is a pretty serious offense and I faced a hefty fine. Years later, I look back and see that having my driving privilege temporarily suspended was actually a good thing for me. Not to mention that the Buick was in deterioration mode, with repair bills staring me down on an almost monthly basis. Finally, I just got fed up. I did the math and calculated that if I just let go of driving—for good—I could free up at least a hundred bucks per month to do things like buy more healthy food, see a movie every once in a while, and not have to fret about constant car problems jacking my checking account.

But beyond the financial savings, I've also had a strong commitment to sustainability. The prerequisite that my workplace be located close to where I live is paramount as I decide on choices for employment. My ethic is that I need to be able to, in a pinch, walk or bicycle to my workplace from home. On my knobby-tired mountain bike, I can pedal to work through woodsy Trinity Park—which has a pretty awesome hike-and-bike trail—in less than 25 minutes. That same distance can be walked (I've done it several times) in about an hour. I love knowing that I am capable of doing this, and don't need to spend money relying on either a personal vehicle or even the limited mass transportation system in my city. I'm good to go with my own two feet and two wheels.

When people comment on how impressed they are that I bicycle everywhere I need to go, I tell them that my bike is my fitness center because I cannot afford to pay to work out at one of those places. They smile and nod, often adding that they wish they had the gumption to do as I do. It's not a brag, it's just the truth: I am too poor to spend money on things that, in an industrialized capitalist society, signify success and maturity. When you're a kid, you bicycle. As an adult, you're supposed to own a car and drive it to the gym.

There were some kids on my block, growing up in south Fort Worth, who seemed to be free-ranging wild children. I think I saw their mother maybe once or twice, but these kids were forever on the street, pedaling their two-wheelers farther away from their house than I was permitted to do. When they came to my end of the street, we circled each other for hours on end and I felt a little whiff of their freedom. They also had the dingiest underwear I'd ever seen, which fascinated me enormously. I couldn't imagine being out on the public streets showing my skivvies that shade of light brown—a color I associate with the Dust Bowl and the hard scrabble life of Americans during the Depression. But these kids didn't have a care in the world, or so it seemed, and the cleanliness of their clothing was the least of their worries.

I think of them sometimes as I bike to the store or to meet a friend at the museum on free day, wearing my non-technical bicycle gear, which in the wintertime often consists of leggings AND sweatpants and three to four layers of top wear: a t-shirt, a wool or cashmere sweater (thrift store, baby), a light jacket, and maybe the faux-down zippered coat. Pedaling along, I am often the most puffed up bicyclist on the trails or streets, resembling the bulky bag lady who wears all the clothing she owns. It's not a pretty sight, but I simply don't want to buy the high-end technical bike garments and accessory gear that are manufactured and marketed for our consumption.

As a bicyclist in 21st century America, I don't care to be corralled into believing that I have to spend lots of money to dress the part of an urban cyclist. I will suit myself, even as it pains me to have to use a backpack to carry my utilitarian necessities (scarves, balaclava, sweater layers) when it becomes too warm to wear them all. I want bicycling in the city to look achievable—get a bike and you're there. You don't have to have the fancy crotch-padded Lycra shorts and hundred dollar handlebar lights. I also don't crave the comments that I sometimes get from cyclists with bigger bank than me. I can tell the intentions are good, it's just in the saying that I am put off.

After a social ride, a guy once commented on my ratty, ripped bicycle seat. I had slipped a black balaclava over it, which was my poor people way of both covering the torn seat and adding more cushioning. He asked, why don't you just buy another saddle? They're only about twenty bucks.

Only. About. It's these two words that hit me hard every time. It's become a loud, resonating indictment uttered by the privileged to the poor: "Money is plentiful and purchasing power is the solution to all problems." Ugh. It's quite shaming, and reveals the absurd assumption that everyone bicycling on your social ride has the same financial capacity as you—or else should surely be trying their damnedest to attain it.

I do make pledges and promises to myself, on the level of money and how I choose to use it, at least once a week. If I just bundle up warmly and pedal on through the ice or mud, I'll reward myself with a coffee from the Java Lab—for not having spent that cash on bus fare to get to work. Or sometimes I pep talk myself, saying, if you bicycle instead of taking a taxi, you can buy yourself a breakfast burrito *and* a coffee. It's a motivational tool for me to get my ass out of bed, onto the bike saddle, and to my destination on my own steam. Ultimately, it is exhilarating to arrive at my workplace, by 6:30am, when it's 28 degrees outside—with the proverbial carrot that had dangled before me now transmuted into a small (but adequate for me) cup of fresh-brewed bistro coffee. This makes my sweaty back, aching calf muscles, and poor state of personal wealth all worth the conscious effort. I'm toning my body while also adjusting my requirements for quality of life and happiness to a scale that is right for me.

I am an artist and practitioner of permaculture principles, which means that I have let go of many belief systems that don't work for me anymore. I also decided long ago that I want to live a life of "voluntary simplicity," which to the uninitiated sounds like I'm saying I want to be poor. Well, voluntary simplicity, on its face, does look like poor. It looks like needy, it looks like barebones living. And to some extent, it is. Practicing voluntary simplicity means I've unsubscribed from blind consumerism and adherence to precepts such as "the more you have, the wealthier you are" or "you can't be in the game if you don't look the part."

I'm a Latina in her early 50s who grew up on Neil Young and Neil Diamond, raised by bilingual U.S.-born parents. I haven't truly "looked the part" of a typical mainstream U.S. citizen since I was born. I'm a bonafide outsider according to the politics and social programming of many citizens that surround me. In a sense, I've been given a license to be different, to not be typical, which allows me freedom to go ahead and live a rebel existence. And I am good with that, because it means that normalizing expectations and restrictive social mores are mine to fuck with— to adapt for my personally-customized palette of aspirations, benchmarks, and measures of success and satisfaction.

I also kind of wish I could find those beige undies kids from my old neighborhood, who grew up white and poor and, hopefully, have made something really awesome of their adult lives. If they were to remember me, even vaguely, maybe they would join me in conversation about those early bike rides together—in the "dangerous" part of town—where we would tear down the streets, unfettered and unconcerned about how we looked as we pedaled towards a horizon of utter joy.

"HOW MUCH DID THAT BIKE COST?"

Gretchin Lair

When I lived with my mom, she taught me to ride without training wheels the same way she taught me to swim by throwing me in the ocean. "Stop crying or I'll give you something to cry about," she said after I fell, and took the bike away. I had a lot of practice being quiet. I learned to sneak into the kitchen to eat peanut butter with my fingers while she was asleep. Otherwise, I would eat nothing at all. When she caught me, she locked me in my room at night.

.   .   .

When I lived with my dad, he played "beat the bank" by writing checks before he had the money to cover them. I taught myself to ride a small bike, one where I could easily put both feet down when I lost balance. The closest house was a mile and a half away on County Farm Road G. When we moved to a house on the highway, I was too scared to bike. So I spent my time singing loudly in large grain silos, climbing hay bale castles, and walking along the big ditch when it was dry.

.   .   .

My college scholarship only covered tuition, so I bounced from couch to couch until I ran out of couches. I rented a large trombone locker from the music department to store blankets and clothes. After the last security check, I would sneak into an unlocked music practice room to sleep until the early students arrived to play piano. I wish I'd had a bicycle then, but it was more important to be invisible than mobile.

·　　·　　·

After college I bought three cheap, unreliable cars in rapid succession. One of them required a special ritual: turn the key, press the starter switch, flip the diesel switch. Every morning I pretended I was performing a solemn ceremony. *Just get me to work on time*, I prayed to gods I didn't believe in.

·　　·　　·

My boyfriend Jacob took me biking once but I couldn't keep up, especially on the last hill. He yelled "Shift! Shift!" as I fumbled with the friction levers. Jacob hated when I didn't listen. He hated when I would walk home alone at night. He really hated when I bought a motorcycle. Everyone loved Jacob, but they didn't see him throw a vacuum cleaner at his sister. They didn't see him chase me through the woods on our anniversary. They didn't see him flip over the coffee table my first day out of the hospital. I kept paying my half of the rent while quietly looking for jobs in other cities.

·　　·　　·

Before I moved, Rob and I met for dinner at our favorite Japanese restaurant. As my oldest friend, I hoped he would be proud of me when I showed him my first reliable car, but he thought I was just showing off. I packed whatever would fit in the back seat and followed the highways west toward a new job, a new life. I sped two days through the desert with the windows rolled down, watching the sun rise and fall and blaze through canyons and parched lands.

·　　　·　　　·

The guys I worked with in San Diego tried to out-do each other at every opportunity: biking, running, drinking, camping, working. Even their sarcasm was competitive. I tried to be like them: I went skydiving; I smoked cigars; I shaved my head. But I was nothing like them and they made sure I knew it.

·　　　·　　　·

Portland was more than I could have hoped for. Not long after I met Sven, I told him that as long as I had a car at least I would always have a place to sleep, a way to escape. But kindness was enough. I never needed to flee. The year after we paid off the car, I found a new bike with shiny ribbons waiting for me on the dining room table. The card read, *Happy Independence Day!*

·　　　·　　　·

I almost vomited after my first bike ride on the Springwater Corridor Trail. I laid on the steps in the garage feeling queasy. I rode up and down hills in our neighborhood at night so nobody would see me panting and struggling. Every mile was progress, but 10 miles all at once seemed as impossible as walking to the moon.

· · ·

The guy at the cycling social laughed. "You want to take *that* bike camping?" he said, waving his hand at my step-through frame and single chain ring. "That's cute." I didn't expect the hill to be so steep and the heat made me cry. But 40 miles later I triumphantly arrived at my yurt. When I left, I boarded a bus to get back up the hill but pedaled the rest of the way home, already planning my next adventures.

· · ·

The year I broke 3000 miles I felt invincible. But I wanted to go farther: longer, higher, faster. To return with stories of emerald forests, snowy mountaintops, wild beaches and foreign countries. To carry the banner of the new year from the golden dawn. To smell the wild roses and greet the twilight cats. I did all that and more, and more.

· · ·

A neighbor stops me. "How much did that bike cost?" she asks. Sven and I live in a colorful house in a beige neighborhood. I ride an expensive folding bike in skirts and coordinated coats. I know the real question is: "How much bike can you afford?" I get asked this question a lot, and no matter what I answer, the response is always the same: "Oh, that's a lot!" *Yes*, I think. *This bike cost me my whole life.*

POEM

Katura Reynolds

It is quite true

that not owning a car

saves my family quite a bit of money

(and gives me the smug satisfaction

of tossing all the car insurance junk mail

directly into the recycle bin)

However

this morning

as the stress of unstable

economies

and wobbly job funding

was preying on my brain

I found myself thinking:

If we lose our jobs

and lose our apartment

—Damn, we wouldn't even have

a car to be living out of, would we?

"HAN"-TED RIDING

Do Jun Lee

THE HAUNTING OF MY FAMILY

I know now that a ghost haunted my family's dinner table. Growing up, my mom prepared sumptuous Korean meals and in response, my siblings and I told her daily that the meal was masisseoyo (맛있어요). But otherwise, silence ruled our meals as if an invisible dinner guest bound our tongues. Or perhaps instead the silence provided for a vacuum that the ghost filled. Perhaps it was a bit of both. As a result, I have only bits and scraps of the life stories of my parents and family. This silence is apparently not uncommon in many immigrant Korean families as Grace Cho writes in *Haunting the Korean Diaspora*:

> The second [Korean] generation, however, having grown up in the United States with neither their parents' storytelling nor a public discourse about the Korean War, told a collective oral history in which they felt affected by some inarticulate presence that had left its imprint on what seemed to be their normal everyday lives. One man said that because of his parents' refusal to talk about their life experiences, their past acted on his present. "For me," he said, "it is not the past. It carries forward into my life. It carries forward into my sisters' lives... as a hole." This experience of

the children of Korean War survivors—having been haunted by silences that take the form of an "unhappy wind," "a hole," or some other intangible or invisible force – reflects the notion that an unresolved trauma in unconsciously passed from one generation to the next.

But now, I am beginning to understand this ghost as a sort of han (한), a Korean word that is most commonly understood as collective transgenerational emotion and experience of unresolved trauma and oppression.

HAUNTED STREETS

I've also come to believe that our streets are haunted by ghosts as well through a sort of past and present collective trauma that remains unresolved. That might appear to be an extreme statement except when you consider the body toll. Since 1899, more than 3.6 million people in the United States have died from car crashes, which is greater than the approximate 2.9 million American soldiers who have died in all American wars. We understand this collective trauma from our fear of the streets, which almost feels instinctual, but rather it's learned and inherited trauma.Enrique Peñalosa observes, "if we tell any three-year-old child who is barely learning to speak in any city in the world today, 'Watch out, a car,' the child will jump in fright, and with a very good reason, because there are more than 10,000 children who are killed by cars every year in the world."[1]

1 Peñalosa, Enrique, "Why buses represent democracy in action" (TED Talk, 20013), www.ted.com/talks/enrique_penalosa_why_buses_represent_democracy_in_action?language=en.

I find it an odd sensation to walk down the middle of a street usually packed with cars that is closed off to traffic for a special event. I always feel a simultaneous sense of unburdened freedom that begins to imagine what streets could be like but also a guilty uncomfortable feeling of transgressing onto a space I'm not really supposed to be in. These ghosts act as a burden, a weight that we can feel. One common way to name our haunting have been ghost bikes, which are often erected to memorialize cyclists who have fallen to motor vehicular violence and to remind us all that cyclists deserve safe travel.

To give a sense of the prevalence of ghosts, Figure 1 is a screenshot from 2011 of the old CrashStat map from Transportation Alternatives of pedestrian and bicyclists fatalities and injuries from car crashes from 1995-2009 in Midtown Manhattan.

The ghosts of car-based trauma haunt every street and corner. We live with past and present trauma in our streets and often have difficulties talking about it as it is normalized into everyday life as blameless forgettable "accidents." But we never truly forget because the damage is written onto our bodies and inscribed into our souls as fear.

HAN

What is han?[2] As mentioned before, han is an indigenous Korean word that describes the collective feelings and experiences of

2 Chang-Hee Son. *Haan of minjung theology and han of han philosophy* (University Press of America, 2000).

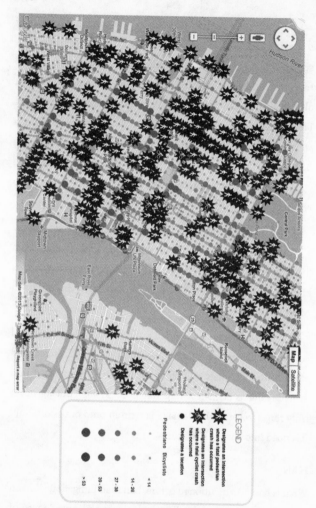

Screenshot of CrashStat: Pedestrian & Cyclist Deaths and Injuries in Midtown NYC

from 1995-2009. (Source: Transportation Alternatives, 2011)

transgenerational trauma. Han is an energy, a force. As such, han facilitates positive or negative energies. In one way, han can be channeled into positive social action and collective movements for justice to resolve oppression. But conversely, han can be channeled as a highly destructive force because of the frustration and desire for revenge that can emerge when a people experience oppression that they do not have the power to resolve. Han can be experienced on personal and collective levels but is rooted at the systematic and structural. However, han has another meaning. The second meaning of han is resolved collective love, which sits in complementary relationship with the other meaning of unresolved collective pain. Thus to resolve collective oppression and trauma, we need to move collectively toward enacted humanity, empathy and love.

THE DMZ

To be Korean also means that we are incomplete, as conflict with North Korea lies in close proximity across a short DMZ that separates us South Koreans from our families in the North. Popular in Korea are the stories of modern-day reunions of family members who had not seen each over several decades. Not long ago, my uncle was reunited for a short meeting with his brother after not seeing him in over 40 years. The story of my hal-meo-ni (할머니 or grandma) haunts me as she was visiting family in North Korea when the DMZ went up and she was stuck on the wrong side. She ended up paying a smuggler to take her on a harrowing trip in a fishing boat along the seacoast back to her home in South Korea. In an alternate reality, I could have been North Korean. Not only are we incomplete, but our North Korea is the shadow part of us but it is also the part that we fear. Our divided country keeps the ghosts alive and wounds open.

INCOMPLETE STREETS

We live in incomplete streets. Many of us drive and a few of us don't. But because of the way we have structured our society, we are all dependent in some degree or another on motor vehicles. For many people, this means that basic needs of daily travel can only be met by the car because our streets and systems of travel have been structured and designed to privilege the car. For others, they may not commute by car, but nearly all of our basic foods and goods are transported by motor vehicles. We are all complicit in car culture and its violence.

At the same time, we all get out of our cars at some point and move as pedestrians, cyclists, skaters, wheelchair users and so on. We are all multi-modal. We are multiple and we are simultaneously both the oppressor and the oppressed in our streets. We embody fear of the street yet we are responsible ourselves for that fear. Maintaining the false divide between drivers and non-drivers feeds the ghosts that keep our streets incomplete. The divide makes it easy for many to blame the victims of car violence rather than look at how we structure our streets. Marginalized bodies also bear the disproportionate brunt of the trauma and pain from incomplete streets.

THE FIRST STEP

About a year and a half ago, Jennifer and I were visiting my parents in LA. Early in my visit, my mom asked us urgently if we would want to see a new Korean film called *Ode to My Father*.

Sensing this was immensely important to my mom, we went to the movie in Koreatown with my parents who cried through much of the movie. This movie was about the dislocation, separation of families, and trauma experienced by Koreans during the Korean War where about 10% of the population (or 3 million people) died. Afterwards, back at home, we spoke with my parents about the movie. My mom plainly said that the movie was their story. My dad, who had rarely if ever spoken about his life in Korea, opened up for the first time about what happened to him. He was a little boy when the war started and he remembered running in the forest, barely dodging the North Korean army. His father and brother were captured and endured forced hard labor for some time until they were released. Even though forced to work for the North Koreans, my dad's family was stigmatized as a result. It was a time of deep poverty and hunger for both my dad and mom's families. This was the first time I ever heard my parents begin to name the ghosts of han that haunted us. **The first step to resolving han is to name our ghosts and our collective pain.**

THE SECOND STEP

"Wait, you're Oriental? But you talk like the rest of us!" exclaimed the print shop owner over the phone.

I had been chatting with this guy for a few minutes about a newsletter we wanted to print and had just given him my name as the person to call back for the estimate. With one hand tensely gripping the phone and my other hand cradling my head to stop from screaming, I calmly replied, "Well, I grew up in California and learned English just like everyone else."

Doubling down, he replied, "But you don't have problems with your Rs and your Ls."

Somehow I managed to laugh it off on the phone and get off the phone as soon as possible. I went over to my coworkers, three white women named Alice, Lucy, and Olga to tell them this amusing anecdote even though I was reeling inside. Instead of laughing, they were appalled and told me in no uncertain terms that we should not give him our business. I tried to say it was okay, but they insisted. Their reaction stunned me in many ways. This was hardly the first time something like this had ever happened to me, but up to this moment, every time I had tried to express my pain to white people, I was told it wasn't that big of a deal. I had grown accustomed to making light of such events and making jokes out of them as a way to tell these stories to whites without enduring a clear rejection of my pain and to fulfill a role of assuaging white discomfort even as I bled inside. But this time was different, as Alice, Lucy, and Olga heard, recognized and validated my experience of pain. I felt loved.

The second step to resolving han is to have our communities acknowledge and validate our oppressions. We can name many of our oppressions (such as Black Lives Matter or Crash not Accident), but we often fight over and protest the lack of the basic recognition of collective wrongs and trauma.

To conclude my story, ironically, when we met with another print shop guy, he had trouble with my name ("Do" pronounced like "doe") to which he replied, "Well, in English, we pronounce your name as 'doo.'" I started to wonder if there was something wrong with all the old white print shop guys in Washington DC.

THE THIRD STEP

In 2012, when I first started biking to midtown Manhattan from Queens, I encountered a dilemma that basically, there was no easy, legal way to get to 2nd Ave on a bike. The fastest, most direct way to get to 2nd Ave is to cut underneath the Queensboro Bridge on 1st Ave and head up on 59th St and hook up with 2nd Ave. The problem for cyclists however is that we have to ride on the sidewalk on 1st Ave as it was a one-way in the opposite direction, and then ride against traffic on 59th St for about half a block. You can see this in a Youtube video[3] from my bike commute in 2012 in this stretch. As seen in Figure 2, the alternatives were to

www.youtube.com/watch?v=aSrH0-jvxwY

ride a long way around (Route 3) or to go a bit less out of your way (Route 2) but encounter dangerous traffic conditions on this stretch of 2nd Ave where cars merge onto the Queensboro Bridge. Like many cyclists, I chose to go the easiest and quickest Route 1 because I could safely and slowly get across on the sidewalk and there was often little oncoming traffic on the part of 59th St where I would bike the wrong way. It wasn't legal, but it wasn't unsafe either as you can see in the video.

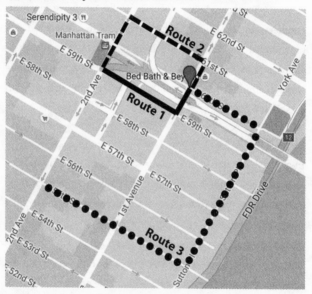

Three options to bike from the Queensboro Bridge to 2nd Avenue towards

downtown.

Riding on the sidewalk and going a bit the wrong way on the street was something I always felt bad and guilty about even as it was safe. There was always a part of me that lived in the fear that the police could at any time issue me summonses and tickets. I wasn't a bad person as I was making the best choice given bad choices, but I could at any moment be marked as a bad person by the police. At the very least, I was certainly often judged as a bad person by pedestrians and drivers. I can't even imagine what it must feel like to be a food delivery cyclist making a countless number of these kinds of decisions every day while physically exhausted and trying to get food delivered quickly.

But then in 2013, the city fixed the problem for cyclists by putting in a connecting bike lane on 1st Ave and a contra-flow bike lane on second half of 59th St. The first time I rode the connecting bike lanes to 2nd Ave, it felt like a minor miracle, my feelings of badness and guilt evaporated. ***This is the 3rd step in resolving han: the community must change structure to resolve collective pain.*** Han cannot be resolved by individual action (like wearing a helmet) or simply recognizing the systematic problems. Not only did the city name and acknowledge our pain, but the city altered the actual structure of the street to resolve the collective problem. You can see this in a Youtube video[4] I took in 2016 of the connecting infrastructure.

Essentially, one day I was doing something illegal albeit harmless and safe, and then the next day, my illegal behavior was codified into legal behavior through a small but meaningful change in infrastructure. This was an act of love by the city

youtube.com/watch?v=vSrNtXTkeaw

towards the cyclists in pain. Han is resolved only through love. This also speaks to the idea that legality is often more about power than it is about preventing harm.

This story also speaks to the power of privilege to resolve han. While a number of working cyclists like the immigrant food delivery workers I have written about have benefited from this bike infrastructure, the process to do so was driven by the more privileged cyclists who commute into midtown Manhattan for white-collar jobs (or academia in my case) on this route. Historically, communities of color have often been ignored when they have asked for street safety improvements. In one case I read about in Melissa Checker's *Polluted Promises*, a city built a highway right in between two black communities. The communities asked for a safe way to cross the highway with a crosswalk and a signal light. Instead the city put in guardrails. The walls that divide and the lack of power to resolve the anguish of han are key features in how han is experienced and traverses generations.

FREEING THE GHOST

"I have bad news. Your baby has no heartbeat on the ultrasound," the doctor solemnly pronounced. Jennifer's sharp gasps and sobs violently pierced my body stunned by disbelief. That same day, my dad went into surgery to remove a life-threatening tumor in his stomach. A few hours after we found out about our lost baby, my sister called to happily tell me about the tremendously successful surgery with my dad in stable recovery. I choked and sobbed out the news about my dead son and did so again when she put my mom on the phone. My mom responded resignedly, "One good thing, one bad thing." I wonder if this response is a side effect from our collective Korean han. We would tell my dad a few days later into his recovery and in his devastation at the news, he sobbed and asked why God would spare his life and not that our baby boy. I tried to assuage him that his health was not connected to the death of my child, but the tears still fell and we all still struggle with feelings of shame and guilt that have no rational basis. Perhaps this is also a residue of han, how easily we can blame ourselves for circumstances beyond our control. All Jennifer and I can do is to hold each other tightly and whisper that we'll get through this together.

About 36 hours later, after an induced labor, Jennifer gave birth to our stillborn boy of 20 weeks into the pregnancy. We named him Rohan, a Sanskrit name, which means "ascending" and also "healing." We had been thinking about boy names with the syllable of han and Rohan just stuck with us. It also sounds like "rowan", which is another common name for mountain-ash, a tree that often shows up in mythology as a symbol of protection. As sweet, tiny Rohan lay still in Jennifer's arms and then mine after the delivery, I felt the echoes of grief from my ancestors before me in a brutal Japanese colonial occupation that sought to erase Korean language and culture, the genocide experienced in the Korean war, and the division of a country (and thus countless families) by more powerful foreign countries. Our family has struggled in silence about these traumas and griefs that haunt us and many others of the Korean diaspora. Zora Neale Hurston once said "If you are silent about your pain, they'll kill you and say you enjoyed it." I think this applies not only to the physical body, but that there can be a kind of murder of your soul through silent suffering (or being forcibly silenced). I write about my personal and our collective grief and trauma as act of love. In this way, I am naming the ghost of Rohan, not so that he'll haunt me, but so that I can set his ghost free as never forgotten and always loved.

RIDING INTO MY HAN

When I bike to the Graduate Center in midtown Manhattan from where I live in Queens, I have to cross and climb the Queensboro Bridge. This climb involves something like a 130 feet within a half mile and on hot muggy summer days, I'm breathing and sweating hard as I pedal. With every leg pump, the N subway train thunders along parallel to me for a moment before disappearing under the river. With each pedal, the East River flows quietly below and while the skyscrapers of Manhattan loom ahead. With each revolution, I'm breathing hard from both East River air on my right and the exhaust of the idling car traffic to my left depending on which way the wind blows. As I struggle and reach the crest of the bridge, I wipe aside the salty streams pouring down my face as my legs burn with something that belongs in the space between pain and joy.

FOUNDING CICLAVIA

Adonia Lugo

We were living in a studio three blocks from the Pacific when Bobby Gadda showed me a video on Streetfilms.org. It was about Bogotá, Colombia's *ciclovía* (bikeway).[5] The nine minute video said that the event closed over 70 miles of streets to car traffic every Sunday, and it seemed to stretch all over the city. Up to two million people biked or walked along the route each week. Aerobics classes and street performances were visible in the film, too, driving home the idea that streets could be more for more than travel. Someone on camera explained the logistics for the event, which unlike a marathon or street festival has crossing points for motorized traffic, making it a "permeable" route. Volunteers and police officers made sure that pedestrians and bicyclists using the ciclovía waited at these crossing points when the lights turned red.

As we watched the video, the gears in my head started grinding. I'd been looking for something like this. In my anthropology graduate program, I was reading theory about the social production of urban environments, and I wanted to find a way to put these ideas to work. My dissertation research would explore why transportation felt the way it did in Southern

5 "Ciclovía: Bogotá, Colombia." Streetfilms, 2007. I was not the only person impressed with the film. When I contacted the filmmaker, Clarence Eckerson, Jr., he said that a number of graduate students had interviewed him about its impact. The ciclovía film was for years the most viewed video on the site.

California. Why did the street feel like a conflict zone? Why did having the money to drive a car make you worth more as a person? What role did culture play in creating and maintaining transportation systems? And, because I wanted to accelerate the transition to sustainable urban living, what could an anthropologist like me do to ease the tension and get more people out in the streets without their cars? The ciclovía offered a real-world example of transforming a mobility space through social activity.

It wasn't lost on me that the event emerged within a latinoamericano urban context. In fact, this was highly relevant for the work I wanted to do. I was born and raised in a Mexican neighborhood in suburban Southern California, and I knew how devalued Latinx culture and the places we made our own could be. Estadounidense anti-immigrant feeling was alive and well in postcolonial California, at least in my native Orange County, and I wondered how this devaluation influenced transportation in less-Republican Los Angeles. Up there, native-born and immigrant Latinxs were some of the most enthusiastic participants in car culture, and also the bulk of people riding buses and trains as what transportation planners call "captive riders." Could this ciclovía thing create a temporary space that disrupted car culture through Latinx means? And, in so doing, could we mix up the captive and the carfree?

I was becoming more and more "carfree" myself, which meant I rode the bus down to school at UC Irvine, and Bobby and I rode the Blue Line train into L.A. when we went into the city. We still had his parents' old Volvo station wagon, but we were using it less and less. Getting around without a car made me feel like I was living in some cool secret world, one with more vibrant colors and sharper edges, but riding a bike could also be a symptom of economic marginality. Just because I considered riding my bike to be a positive thing didn't mean everyone out there, like the men of color riding mountain bikes on sidewalks, felt the same way. Was there some way to connect carfree people like me with these other folks who already had a lived sense of what it was like to get around without a car (but maybe wished they didn't)?

A Colombian street happening seemed like a good vehicle for exploring these questions building up on my research to-do list, so Bobby and I flew to Bogotá in mid-August 2008. The city was damp and green, with an overcast sky. 9,000 feet in the Andes, Bogotá has a temperate climate and sees drizzly rain year round. We wandered around the city for three weeks and I never totally adjusted to the narcotic effect the high altitude had on my body. The tiny *tintos* of coffee available everywhere didn't pack the punch of the large cups I'd been hooked on since going to college in the Pacific Northwest.

We stayed with various hosts and learned about local architecture, public cultural resources, and national history. We attended three ciclovías, but beyond those Sundays, we saw few bicyclists using the extensive network of *ciclorutas*, bike paths crisscrossing the city. We saw few bicyclists braving dense, swift traffic in narrow, winding streets. We saw few bicyclists in the hip neighborhoods. Nobody we met had two bikes to lend us for the ciclovía, and no shop offered bicycle rental we could afford. Many of the bikes we did see in use were cargo bikes used to haul scrap for recycling, to vend food, or for other trade purposes. These were too wide to fit between the ciclorutas' occasional bollards. Street vendors offered bike parts on blankets, alongside replacement blender parts, but it seemed like the blenders everyone used to make fresh fruit smoothies were more common than bicycles.

Smelly air pollution made it clear why the ciclovía was popular in a diesel city, and so did the traffic. I saw it thicker in Bogotá than ever before. The cars were smaller than in California, which meant congestion was composed of tiny sedans zooming forward in short bursts. Drivers did not yield to pedestrians. Crossing the street meant running unless you were part of a throng. There were no pauses and waves, friendly gestures of road sharing. Motorbikes were more common than bicycles. Taxi drivers were known to run red lights. All in all, removing motorized traffic really changed the character of the street.

Besides the Sunday street closures, another method for improving air quality was "pico y placa," a system that used vehicle registration to determine who could drive on what days. One host told us that people would love to drive more and resented these limits. This surprised me, since the stance I was starting to understand among sustainable transportation advocates in the U.S. was that they thought they could convince everyone to *choose* to use cars less. In this city that was getting global attention, transportation was impacted by autocratic measures we weren't likely to be able to implement in Los Angeles. It wasn't a city full of happy people joyfully choosing to walk, bike, and ride the bus. It was full of people who might like to drive more but couldn't because of congestion, regulations, and expense.

Given these contrasts, I might have been discouraged from trying to import the ciclovía, if I hadn't met someone who could explain to me how it grew from an idea into its present form: Jaime Ortiz Mariño. We met with Jaime at the Bogotá *alcaldía* (mayor's office), where he was minister of domestic transportation. As part of the PRO-CICLA group that also included Fernando Caro Restrepo and Rodrigo Castaño Valencia, Jaime founded the ciclovía in 1974 after returning to Bogotá from undergraduate studies at Case Western Reserve University in Cleveland.

It hadn't been a straight line from 1974 to 2008; the events had actually waxed and waned over the years. But in 1994, Antanus Mockus, a university professor and administrator, ran a successful and unconventional campaign for mayor. Once in charge, he used unusual tactics to improve civic culture in the city, such as hiring mimes to mock aggressive motorists and sponsoring a "women's night." The ciclovía grew under Mockus, who used humor and play to build community.

When I asked Jaime via email in May 2013 if the street closures were a means to improve public space and street safety in Bogotá, Jaime clarified that, "in the center [of PRO-CICLA], the bicycle was the symbol and the ciclovía was the instrument we came up with, to open the debate on urban processes and urban form in Colombia in the seventies. Urban safety, betterment of public space, community health and recreation, generation of urban consciousness, development of social integration, etc., were also aims of the event, today proven as end results of the process." Closing the street was an action seen to have impacts far beyond transportation.

At our meeting, Jaime made photocopies of some newspaper articles from the 1970s covering the early ciclovías. He also made sure I understood the postcolonial significance of a transportation idea from South America taking hold in the United States. Colombia followed American highway designs, approximating modernity through automobile infrastructure. But now, Americans were looking to Colombia for alternatives. He sketched me a map of the world that showed what he called the "global center" (as opposed to "global south") as the "unión de naciones asoleadas" (Union of Sunny Nations). Instead of us sending car culture to Colombia via highway engineering, as had been the trend, they were modernizing us by sending a carfree event north; as Jaime put it, *we* were the "provincianos," and they were "universalizing" us.

Jaime's emphasis on postcolonial disruption appealed to me as an alternative to the eurocentric vision I was finding in bike media that preached European street design like a gospel. It made a lot more sense to me to try and map a *bogotano* model onto Los Angeles than it did to fantasize about overlaying a Danish or Dutch street culture there. I left Bogotá convinced that we should give a ciclovía a shot in L.A. and take our place in the Union of Sunny Nations. By October, Bobby and I were part of a ciclovía organizing committee in central Los Angeles.

We'd attended a board meeting of the Los Angeles County Bicycle Coalition (LACBC) about a week after getting back to the states, where we met traffic engineer Stephen Villavaso. When the topic of a ciclovía committee came up, it turned out he was also interested in starting something. The next day, LACBC's executive director, Jen Klausner, started an email list for people interested in starting a ciclovía in L.A. Bobby and I wrote a report about our visit to Bogotá and speculated as to how a ciclovía might look in Los Angeles. We sent it to the ciclovía list, which had grown to include people beyond LACBC interested in the concept.

Soon after, the committee had its first meeting at Allison Mannos' apartment in East Hollywood. Along with Bobby, Stephen, Allison, and me, the organizers from that meeting who stayed on with the effort were environmentalists Jonathan Parfrey and Sandra Hamlat. Jonathan had also seen the ciclovía Streetfilm, and had been circulating it to his networks for some time. He had a long history of work in anti-nuclear and water activism and had much more experience than the rest of us in organizing, policy, and fundraising. Sandra worked in conservation policy. We were joined at subsequent meetings by Colleen Corcoran, a graphic designer and Stephen's partner.

We met as volunteers on a monthly basis, and our meetings maintained a non-hierarchical structure. Stephen and Sandra framed it to me later as a "meeting of equals," where everyone contributed differently. Our core committee combined people who knew how to navigate the waters of policy and fundraising and people with the technical skills to make the idea seem more possible. Stephen could design a route study that would make sense to engineers with the city; Colleen and her collaborator Joseph Prichard turned our brainstorming into a graphic style.

The committee was dedicated to including a range of bicycle users in the event by closing streets in multiethnic central L.A., rather than starting in a more eco-friendly but racially homogeneous city such as Santa Monica. Along the same lines, we hoped to get the city on board to make our event "official" because that would make a bigger statement than just another group bike ride or protest march.

Picking a name came first. We weighed the pros and cons of tweaking an already unfamiliar term and issues of pronunciation. Other cities had created new names to describe their events, such as Summer Streets in New York City and

Sunday Parkways in Portland. Nine messages into an email thread on the ciclovía committee list, Stephen brainstormed, "Via of Ciclovia means a passage or a way thru. The meaning of Ciclovia is of basic elements. How about retaining most of it and call it CicLAvia. When you search CicLAvia, google asks if you meant 'ciclovia.' That could be good." We went with Stephen's suggestion, and started getting in touch with other U.S. cities holding ciclovía-style events.

At our next meeting in December, we discussed how to bring more activists into the effort, benefiting from Jonathan's many years of experience in organizing and environmental advocacy in Los Angeles. Jonathan emphasized that many people were becoming aware of bicycle and pedestrian infrastructure issues: transportation people, parks people, even economic forecasters. In terms of community involvement, Jonathan advised, we needed to go neighborhood by neighborhood. For the MacArthur Park area, maybe we should reach out to immigration advocacy groups. Target groups according to the neighborhoods our route would pass through, including neighborhood councils. Always, Jonathan cautioned, be respectful of groups who see themselves as gatekeepers. He started a shared document where we built a list of the groups we might need to include in planning.

Jonathan suggested creating a visual rendering of what the ciclovía would look like, creating images of bicycles in front of recognizable landmarks. We decided to put together a presentation about the trip Bobby and I had taken to Bogotá that incorporated Stephen's maps and Colleen's graphics. Our language framed the event as creating a temporary park space as a response to Los Angeles' "park poor" status. We also started strategizing funding possibilities for our ciclovía, planning to send "letters of inquiry" to public health foundations. Public health would be an important component of the event. We talked about framing the event as a way to stimulate demand for bicycle infrastructure, a strategy that would increase our eligibility for federal transportation funding coming into the city.

Our first route-scouting ride was in mid December 2008. Bobby, Stephen, Colleen, Sandra, and I met at MacArthur Park and biked west on Wilshire Boulevard toward LACMA. Stephen and I took notes on sites that might be negatively impacted by a Sunday street closure, such as churches with parking lots that only opened onto Wilshire, and potential allies, such as cultural organizations. We scanned each block and thought about ways an eco-friendly dry cleaner, or a Korean radio station, or an empty plaza at the base of a corporate tower might be transformed by crowds of bicyclists. Through our eyes, this heavily congested, car-dominated stretch of Los Angeles became a riverbed where we could see a flood of people biking and walking. A flood that would grow from the steady trickle of people already biking and walking on the sidewalks of Wilshire.

There was a lot of logistical planning to be done around event insurance, political support, and fundraising, deciding whether to plan our own event without city support, deciding whether to try to take over a "name" street like Sunset or Wilshire. These could be fun conversations, especially as people lobbied for routes that included their personal favorite symbols of Los Angeles. Each of us wondered, what would be the most transformative route that allowed people to see the same L.A. differently? Unlike the group rides popular in L.A. at that time, where one or two bicyclists stand in the middle of intersections and hold back traffic to allow everyone to ride through red lights, our route would be permeable to cars like in Bogotá. Joe Linton joined the CicLAvia effort after seeing a presentation at the Los Angeles Bike Summit in March 2009. He became a core organizer of the event. Joe brought a tremendous amount of knowledge about bike policy and grassroots bike networks in L.A., something we had been lacking.

To start sharing our idea with the public, we held a ciclovía workshop at artist and urban designer James Rojas' gallery, g727, in June 2009. James uses model-building as a tool for accessing community members' knowledge about the environments they inhabit, and at this workshop he asked participants to create what they considered to be a bike-friendly street. One attendee was a Colombian-Puerto Rican artist named Carolina Caycedo who had a show up in the gallery. She spoke enthusiastically about growing up with ciclovía, and talked about the lively social space it gave to teens for flirting and preening. Carolina's interactive art show centered on exchange, and she sought to tie different people together through things they offered each other. I envisioned CicLAvia as just this sort of connection space. Traffic infrastructure tends to eliminate instances when road users interact with each other directly, in the name of efficiency and safety. I wanted to give traveling together a positive spin with a party in the street.

Jonathan and Sandra were both networked with people who worked for the city, so Sandra contacted her acquaintance Romel Pascual, a deputy to Mayor Antonio Villaraigosa, and other friends about CicLAvia. By now, our goal was to make the ciclovía into a weekly, city-run program with permanent street signage along a route that would expand over time. Through our communications with other cities experimenting with ciclovías, such as Portland, Chicago, New York, and Miami, we learned that we were the only city in the U.S. to start with a grassroots ciclovía campaign. All other cities' events came from planners who thought it sounded like a good idea. We made sure to emphasize the role of city support in these other places when we met with the mayor's staff.

Getting the city on board took time for a number of reasons. City employees are middle-class residents of this region, meaning they likely view traveling outside of a car with the same contempt most people do. Politicians don't have much incentive to support non-car transportation projects, since most of their constituents care a lot about their own car-based commutes and because directing resources to those who aren't driving can be seen as helping the wrong people.

We were still working on getting city support in May 2009, when a friend directed me to a new issue of *Los Angeles Magazine* where experts had offered suggestions to the mayor about the future of L.A.. One person, Aaron Paley of an art events company called Community Arts Resources (CARS-LA), suggested a ciclovía. I emailed him and told him about CicLAvia, and he responded enthusiastically. Aaron was headed to Bogotá that month, so I also sent an email connecting him with Jaime Ortiz Mariño so he could hear the same vision Bobby and I had. By July, the CicLAvia committee was meeting at CARS' offices in the Wiltern Building at Wilshire and Western. As an experienced event planner, Aaron helped the committee focus our efforts on political support and fundraising.

We secured Mayor Antonio Villaraigosa's tentative support that fall, but political will shifted further in our favor in December 2009. That month, Mayor Villaraigosa attended the United Nations Climate Change Summit in Copenhagen, which brought politicians from all over the world to what bike advocates consider the model city for bike infrastructure. While there, a radio show interviewed him, and the host asked him what plans L.A. had to promote bicycling. Villaraigosa alluded to a street closure event that was in the works. Even though he did not mention our effort by name, this was a big deal because it was the first time he had publicly acknowledged his support for CicLAvia. This meant we could represent our future event to potential funders as city-sanctioned.

In January 2010, we started meeting with city staff to plan the logistics of our first event, which would allow us to get a firm estimate of how much the event would cost. At this point, our proposed route included thirteen miles of streets. Things moved slowly because staff from the Department of Transportation (LADOT) and the Bureau of Street Services were uninterested and skeptical. Even though we had the mayor's support, these bureaucrats had their reasons for resisting working with us. In one meeting, a supervisor from LADOT told us that, "the streets were made for parking and travel. They weren't made for an event." Several times staff mentioned a horrific incident in which an elderly man drove a car into a pedestrianized space in Santa Monica and did not brake before killing multiple people.

More recently, a bicyclist riding on a closed route during a triathlon had sued the city for damages after a motorist drove onto the route and struck him, leaving him partially paralyzed. The rumor was that this exercise in liability cost the city millions and made them adamant that we must have at least six traffic safety officers at each intersection where traffic would cross the route. Paying off-duty officers overtime wages would make our event much more expensive than we had anticipated, and this was one reason the event got cut down from thirteen to seven and a half miles.

Another reason was that city staff responsible for estimating the costs of the street closure did not want to provide an estimate for the full route we initially proposed. Citing limited work hours, the city worker assigned to help us with logistics said he could only cost out a seven and a half mile route. Later an LADOT traffic engineer rejected a section of the proposed route that would divert motorists from a surface street onto a highway, informing us that, "we don't force people to get on the freeways. Some people don't feel comfortable driving on the freeway." The message was that LADOT recognized that people might fear driving, but accommodated this through keeping surface streets open to them rather than improving conditions for bicyclists and pedestrians. Negotiating with the city further proved the need for an event that gave people the opportunity to feel comfortable outside of their cars on city streets, and it gave me a lot of good stories for my dissertation project.

Through the spring of 2010, even as we were meeting with city staff to plan logistics for the event, the mayor's office lagged in giving us an official letter of support that we could take to funders, or to guarantee that they would pay for half of the event's expenses. As the months wore on and we started sharing our October 10 target date with the public, we remained apprehensive that the city would renege and leave us with an event we could not fund. But then the mayor crashed his bike.

Villaraigosa sometimes engaged in the high-status pastime of recreational cycling, taking long rides through L.A. on weekends. On one such ride, as he was traveling in a bike lane on congested Venice Boulevard in Culver City, a motorist pulled out in front of him. Startled, Villaraigosa crashed his bike and ended up with a sprained shoulder. When the news broke, the L.A. bike movement stood up and shouted a collective, "I told you so!" regarding the city's poor biking conditions. In response, Villaraigosa had his aides plan a "mayor's bike summit" where all of us could come to the Metro headquarters and air our grievances for 90 seconds apiece. Word spread through the bike community on blogs, at meetings, and via flyers. The mayor's bodily entanglements in Copenhagen and on Venice Boulevard became significant milestones for CicLAvia. 10-10-10 was on.

Once we had a firm date, the CicLAvia committee started becoming part of a political machine. We were invited to speak at the mayor's bike summit, and Aaron and I showed up armed with t-shirts and a quick presentation. Many people in the room already knew about CicLAvia. "I was already supporting this event before the accident," the mayor assured the standing-room only audience, crammed in with their messenger bags and helmets. In that moment, CicLAvia provided the evidence he needed to show that he was responding to these constituents' concerns.

The first CicLAvia closed seven and a half miles of streets in Los Angeles from 11 am until 3 pm on Sunday, October 10, 2010. An estimated 30-40,000 people rode bikes or walked along the route, which passed from historically Latino Boyle Heights in East L.A. through Little Tokyo and Downtown L.A., into Central American MacArthur Park and Koreatown, ending at East Hollywood's Bicycle District, a hub for the cycling community in central Los Angeles. Jaime had come up from Bogotá for the event, and was one of the speakers at the press conference the mayor held at the Boyle Heights end of the route. It was nice to see his role as a visionary recognized.

There have been at least two CicLAvia events each year since its first iteration on October 10, 2010, and it has shifted routes to connect new parts of the city through close collaboration with community-based organizations. We'd grafted a bogotano event onto the Angeleno landscape and the hybridization took, to the surprise of many. At each CicLAvia I've attended, I've enjoyed the crowded bottlenecks where so many people have shown up that we have to walk our bikes, and the long stretches in between where I can ride fast and the street is quiet.

In a way, I never saw CicLAvia realized. I left L.A. within a few months of 10-10-10, and while other co-founders moved on to closer relationships with local government agencies, I cloistered myself and spent several years analyzing it all a thousand miles away in Seattle. By the end, I was more interested in questions of diversity in bicycle advocacy than I was in promoting a particular intervention like CicLAvia. I'd gone to college in the Pacific Northwest, and in returning to write my dissertation there, I saw in stark relief what I'd only seen surfacing occasionally in Los Angeles' sea of multiracial and multicultural urban movements: plenty of people advocate for bicycling without seeing a need to disrupt the racism and classism that are part and parcel of how we plan and use land. So there's a version of CicLAvia that has lived mainly in my head and in my publications, an old nexus of relationships pickled in a jar for further study, and that's what you've read here.

IVY CITY DREAMS

Phill Melton

ormer Department of Transportation director: there's no bike infrastructure Over There because the residents never asked for it.

Residents of Over There: you want to help us build new bike infrastructure? We've been asking for that for years, and nobody's ever listened!

.   .   .

The shop I work at is opening a new location. Most of our customers haven't heard of the neighborhood it's in, fewer know where that neighborhood is, and almost none of them can tell you how to get there. Granted, there really aren't any good ways to bike there—something about being hemmed in between highways and railroad tracks.

It's not a place too many people ever thought about, except as an object lesson in the effects of recession, neglect, and urban poverty. For years it was the city's dumping ground, home to motor pools, warehouses, and homeless shelters. Well, there was that one nightclub that kept getting shut down every few months and changing its name. Oh, and the speed cameras on the road out of town that kept catching people going 20 over. But nobody lived there, right? Just some loafers who didn't maintain their houses, I guess.

Then the distillery opened. Then the brewery. Another distillery. Then the yoga studio, the crossfit gym, the athletic clothing store, and the bike shop. Oh, the organic grocery, coffee roaster, and another (!) distillery. Can't forget the luxury apartments. Bouldering gym's set to open soon, along with the food incubator.

Now people are wondering when the bridge over the tracks is going to be built.

· · ·

As a colleague put it once, it really sucks having to follow passion and fire, sharing how cycling changed our lives, connected us with our world and our neighbors, gave us freedom, with "and that'll be $2,000, please."

· · ·

Everyone knows what a stolen bike looks like. It's beat up, covered in filth, with mismatched parts and completely the wrong size for the rider. There's probably some jury-rigged system for carrying things on it, since the original bike was never meant for transit. Ask, and you'll hear some story about how the current owner got it from an uncle, or a friend, or paid $100 for it.

At this point, "that bike's too big for you" is pretty much what my colleagues say to me instead of "good morning." I'm not completely sure how my rack stays attached to Valentine—some bodge I cooked up involving a carriage bolt and epoxy—and about half his parts were takeoffs from (other, nicer) late '80s road bikes.

We're not even going to go into that somewhat shameful layer of street grime that covers the nicks, scratches, exposed steel, and rust on his frame.

Nobody's ever questioned that I bought him for $5 at a campus police auction.

.　　.　　.

"What are they protesting?"

"Oh, the landlord's trying to evict them and build more condos, but they're filing an injunction to stop him. There's a pretty good article in the *Post* about it."

"But they have to face the facts: the neighborhood's changed. They should move to the suburbs to be with their own kind; the services they need just don't exist here."

Like Hell they don't. The bakery next door serves them. The barber shop in the building they live in serves them. So long as I'm here, I serve them.

.　　.　　.

I'm pretty sure that, at this point, I'm part of the tribe of bikeshopminions who Just Don't Get American capitalism. I mean, I've read Adam Smith, have a decent grasp of economics, follow the business section of the paper, can keep a ledger, that sort of thing—but can't for the life of me understand, in metaphysical terms, what *exactly* a mortgage-backed security is or what's so vital about repackaging them.

Should mention that I used to teach metaphysics. "Understanding things in metaphysical terms" used to be part of my job description. Was pretty good at that job, if I do say so myself.

But somehow, manipulating these metaphysically nebulous...things...is absolutely crucial to the continued functioning of our society. It's crucial and valued in a way the knowledge and ability of my friend the old-school bike courier— you know, the guy who gets called when someone needs 541 copies of a report delivered downtown within the hour because he and his trailer are faster and more efficient than any truck, who knows where to find every art car and crazy front yard sculpture garden in town, who will gladly tell you the best way to bike over any hill within a hundred miles of his house—isn't.

That I'll never understand.

· · ·

Other things I'll never understand: how a complete klutz like me can suddenly turn graceful when on a bike; the fullness of the deep and mystical connection between coffee and cycling; where exactly all those bike caps came from; why I don't take the way home that has the amazing view of the Basilica as I climb every night.

Things I might understand: that it's impossible not to groove at a stoplight when the car stereo next to you is playing go-go; how hard it is to fight the control freak's urge to grab both brakes when diving down MLK Avenue from St. Liz's, dodging potholes and erratic drivers, rack shaking over the cracks in the pavement, knowing it's worth it for the wind, the feeling of passing effortlessly through the city, gliding past the Big Chair and down to the river; how it's almost always worth it to take the back alley, to see a different side of the world than the street view.

•   •   •

A new shop can be...well, clinical. Intimidating. Off-putting, even. All sparkly and new, a swank boutique, a shrine for objects—and not a place for life. It doesn't matter how friendly and welcoming you are if the environment makes people fret about intruding on such a hermetically perfect space by bringing their messy, real, and living selves into it.

Wood, concrete, and glass don't drip melting sleet, sweat, and snot as they walk in the door. They don't have odd jiggly bits they've always hated, they can be reconfigured to look oh-so-perfect, ever-so-tasteful, just like they should be, an ideal rational order, always ready for the photo shoot.

Perfection is forever frozen. It can't improve, it can't change. It's dead. Frankly, it's boring.

Cycling is kinetic, empowering, liberating, slightly crazy, a gift to the eternally imperfect. It's life-giving, life-affirming.

So I've started collecting bits of life for when we move in. A wall mounted bottle opener here, an odd paperweight there, and lots and lots of stickers. Some from my bike activist friends, some from places you can bike to from our front door, many with personal stories, even one that's hand-drawn. Anything to have a touch of anarchy, of wit and humor, a personal touch, a bit of change, or perhaps just a sign that living people have been here and all are welcome.

It'll take years—decades!—before the place feels Right, before the stories told and lives lived in this space begin to permeate the walls and seep out of the floor. A living space— with its histories, smells, and personalities—can't be created overnight, but it might be able to have a good start and a little encouragement.

·　　·　　·

One of my side gigs is installing bike parking. Six staple racks, a box of bolts, and half a ton of tools loaded into a kid trailer that shows its years of adventures past, and off we go! Pull up to our site, four holes drilled through the concrete, four bolts sunk, one staple bound to the streetscape, and someone locks up almost before we've moved our tools. There on the sidewalk, in front of law firms and lobbyists, we're just another pair of workers nobody really notices, blending in with the city's scenery and noise.

Well, except for that one time we installed the racks by the homeless shelter. Then we had a constant stream of people coming by to thank us.

·　　·　　·

Whenever I come to work, my ride takes me from the streetcar suburb where I live, through towns whose times have come and gone and come again, along rivers and roads used by natives and invaders, farmers and urbanites. Neighborhoods merge into neighborhoods, stream valleys give way to ridgelines, and, at the very end, the bike path lines up perfectly with the scaffolding-clad dome of the Capitol before turning right into a network of new glass-and-steel canyons.

Why do I do it? Well, it saves a few dimes living out here, sure, and I tell myself riding in is free (aside from that espresso habit). But really, I'd miss that feeling of sliding between towns and neighborhoods, of the way each place feels at each moment, how those shades of feeling and character imperceptibly change and change again as I keep riding.

I'd miss my city, my home, if I saw less of it, if I felt less of it, if I knew less of it.

.   .   .

The local Department of Transportation held a public meeting on a proposed bike lane a while back. It could have gone better. Words were exchanged. The police had to break up the meeting an hour early, ostensibly because the meeting room was over capacity.

Now, I'm not exactly the type who believes that bicycle infrastructure is a cancer, as one resident put it, but I understand why people view this as an amenity for Someone Else, an attempt to destroy their neighborhoods and communities in favor of wealthier, whiter newcomers. Talk about "The Plan" to displace long-term residents may sound like paranoid nattering, but it's happened before.

Swampoodle used to be an Irish neighborhood, before it was removed to put in the train station. The Italian neighborhood near Judiciary Square had a freeway run through it, a canyon that blighted the surrounding blocks. Chinatown—half-jokingly called "Chinablock" nowadays—had the convention center plopped on top of it, the residents run off to the suburbs. Already suffering due to the '68 riots, the street closures and disruption from long-delayed Metro construction killed many of the remaining businesses in Shaw. Residents of a neighborhood along the waterfront, near the fish market, were evicted and relocated to housing projects east of the river; in their place went acres of lifeless and soul-destroying brutalist concrete, a non-neighborhood that precisely conveys the character of the bureaucracy that spawned it.

All in the name of urban renewal, the city beautiful, and clearing the slums.

So when I see new bike routes being planned in a long-ignored part of the city, now that the Great White Antiseptic Foodie Pop-Up Market has arrived—conveniently displacing the old Italian market that had been there for eighty years, rich with the smell of spices, sausages, hardwood floor, and generational memory—I wonder. When people complain that bike lanes are only going in to encourage them to get out, I understand. When I see research from my advocacy colleagues showing that bike infrastructure leads to the mixed blessing of increased property values, I worry that this will benefit only the privileged, but harm those we ought to protect. When a new bike shop—*my* shop!—opens in a rapidly gentrifying neighborhood, I fear for the results.

I can't change the past, nor the hard, bitter lessons people have drawn from it. Time and again, services and infrastructure that ought to be for everybody have been used to displace and destroy, then encourage the privileged and powerful to colonize. There are good reasons people perceive this.

I can, however, fight the injustices and inequalities that have caused these perceptions. I can work for equity, for a better way forward, for the radical idea that all people deserve safe, affordable, and effective transit. I can make it clear that these things are for all people—we're not meeting you halfway, we're not stooping to your level, we're welcoming you, the real and present you of this moment, this place is yours, *you belong here*.

WHEN VALUES COLLIDE

Julie Brooks

I walked into the town hall meeting expecting to be educated on, and show my support for, a bike boulevard plan being rolled-out, the result of a five-year collaborative effort between our local bicycling alliance, the neighborhood association and city council. By the time I'd been sitting in my seat for roughly five minutes, and before the meeting even began, I was helplessly seething with rage at the reminder of the individualism and isolation that existed in the room. The following is the transcript of a dialogue I overheard between two women sitting right in front of me. Though I missed the beginning of this conversation as I settled myself, the portion below provides a stark example of the chasm that continues to be perpetrated by people with narrowly defined and stereotypical social class values and agendas regarding transportation and accessibility.

Beth (B):   "Why don't you drive a car?"

Christine (C):   "I don't want to drive a car. I ride a bike."

B: "But, you could get a car."

C: "I don't want a car. I ride a bike."

B: "Who doesn't want a car? Bikes are so slow. Don't you work? Or, are you just one of those freaks who likes to get a lot of exercise?"

C: "I work, and I ride a bike."

B: "You must work really close to your house."

C: "Actually, I ride my bike 30 miles a day. 15 miles each direction."

B: "Bet it takes you forever to get to work. Why don't you have a car?"

C: "I don't want a car. I ride a bike."

B: "Oh, you can find a car cheap. Did you look on Craig's List?"

C: "I don't want a car. I ride a bike."

B: "But, cars are cheap. 'specially if you buy a used one. My brother-in-law sells used cars. Seriously, tell him I sent you."

C: "What about the gas and insurance? And, the maintenance costs?"

B: "Well, you gotta have gas, unless you buy one of those Hybrids or somethin'. But I hear those aren't reliable."

C: "And, insurance? Maintenance?"

B: (Whispering into C's ear) "Do you know how many people don't have insurance?"

C: "I don't need a car. I ride a bike."

B: "Where did you get your bike?"

C: "At the Bicycle Coop."

B: "Coop? That's not a bike shop, is it?"

C: "No, it's a coop. People donate bikes, or bike parts, they're not using anymore, or, maybe find on the street. Then volunteers fix them up for people who need or want a bike."

B: "Oh, so it's a charity. Your bike must not be a new bike."

C: "Well, it was new to me when I got it six years ago."

B: (Again, in a hushed tone) "So, you can't afford a car? (Then, in a more audible tone) "Can I make a donation to that bike charity? I haven't made enough donations yet this year."

C: The Coop isn't really a charity, per se. But, I guess you could make a donation."

B: "How does it work? I mean, if they give bikes away to poor people isn't that a charity?""

C: "Well, if someone wants a bicycle they have to go through a program to learn how to take care of their bike, and ride their bike safely. They also have to volunteer a certain number of hours to earn their bike. It's not just for poor people, but it really does help to make sure that those who want a bike for transportation can get one."

B: "Well, poor people do have a lot of time on their hands, right? So, it makes sense that they should learn how to take care of something. I want a new bike. Can you recommend a good shop?"

C: "No. I volunteer at the Coop and take care of my bike there."

B: "But, don't you have to take your bike somewhere when you need something fixed."

C: "Nope. I can do most things by myself."

B: "So, you're a bike mechanic. Is that your job? No wonder you ride your bike to work."

C: "No, I'm not a bike mechanic. Or, at least that's not my day job."

B: "What do you do?"

C: "About what?"

B: "For work? What do you do for work?"

C: "I do help out at the Coop. That's where I learned how to take care of my bike."

B: "I don't need to know how to take care of my bike. I just want a good, reliable bike to ride on the bike paths with my kids. (After a brief pause) Do you ride on the road? I hate cyclists who ride on the road. They slow everybody down, and one of these days one of them's gonna get killed."

C: "Lots of bicyclists have already been killed."

B: "Probably because they didn't stop for a stoplight like they should. Do you ride on the road?"

BICYCLE KARMA

Rebecca Fish Ewan

In 1969, we arrived in Berkeley at night before the power was turned on in the rental house—my single dad, me, and my three siblings. Seated on boxes in the dark, we felt out of place, accustomed as we were to living in the country along the dirt road where I'd learned to ride a bike. Everything had changed when my mom left, and now we were going to live in a big city on food stamps and any coins dropped in the basket on the ground in front of my dad's classical street quartet. He played the harpsichord he'd built from oak and plywood, just the right size to fit into his VW van and roll out onto Maiden Lane in San Francisco. Once or twice, I went with him to turn pages as he plinked out Bach while finely-dressed people streamed by on their way to Macy's.

Back then, being broke was our full time job and my dad was always trying to offer us ways to get by and have fun without money—free yoga, free museum day at the De Young, free dinner at the Hari Krishna temple, a day spent helping build People's Park, or baking fifty loaves of bread for the food co-op. I liked his idea of fun, but it could be a bit serious. When I needed plain old kid fun, I'd hop on my pale blue one-speed Schwinn and pedal along the sidewalk and dip onto a quiet street to meander for hours through the neighborhood. An afternoon like this wouldn't cost me a dime, unless I rode up to Bott's for a double-scoop of orange sherbet. My favorite ride was down a steep hill on a tree-lined street, up where the rich people lived and the trees grew so big their canopies touched to form a tunnel of leaves above the street. Cars barely ever drove by in the afternoon, so I'd hog the whole road, point my bike down hill and pedal like mad. Once I hit top speed, I'd toss my head back and swing my legs out to the sides, so the warm afternoon breeze could dance my sneakered feet around. I'd watch the leaves whizzing above my head, dappled green blurring into the brilliant blue sky, no sound but the wind whiffling across my ears. Pure free joy.

By the time I hit my teens, that bike was long gone, stolen, I think, from the side of the house. Berkeley was a town full of bike thieves. Without wheels, I had to make the mile walk to high school on mornings I overslept and missed the bus, which was just about every morning. My dad had fallen in love and moved to Oregon, but I stayed behind in the duplex he had somehow managed to buy and hang onto after he left. I lived with my older sister in the upstairs flat. My dad's ex-girlfriend took the downstairs and gave me twenty bucks a week, a kind of partial rent for being able to stay in my dad's house long after they had split up. A complicated arrangement that left me hungry and without a bike.

Spring of my freshman year, one of my classmates asked me and another girl to help her with a poster contest that had a $1,000 cash prize. The only glitch was it was a contest for veterans. The girl's uncle was a vet, but he didn't like to color, so he had given the poster to her. I think he wanted 10%, if it won. We tried to make up for the wrongness of what we were doing by coloring the shit out of that poster. Despite spending a week covering every square inch with flair pen colors, I can't remember much about what it looked like. When I draw, I tend to lean down till my nose nearly touches the paper, so I barely looked at the full image. Perhaps I also can't recall it clearly because the memory is cloaked with guilt. The contest theme was Veterans and Hope, or some similar uplifting sentiment. I can still picture just those words, a bouquet of flowers, and maybe a rainbow.

After my friend sent off our entry, I figured that was the end of it. After all, cheaters can't be winners. That's not how the world works. I resumed over-sleeping and walking to school. Until the afternoon when I came home to find out we had won first place and the $1,000 bucks, which seemed like a fortune to me. My cut was enough for me to buy a brand new Peugeot ten speed, a chain and padlock. Someone snapped a photo of me the day I bought the bike, standing in the front yard in cutoffs and a halter top, hanging onto the handlebars, grinning like a circus monkey. I guess I mitigated my shame for cheating with the glee I felt in owning a brand new bicycle, a bike that I never could have afforded on my weekly twenty buck allowance.

I joined the high school biking club and in sophomore year we toured down the coast from Morro Bay to San Diego, a gaggle of teens and our weary science teacher, all on bikes, carrying everything we needed for camping. No wimpy sag wagon for us. We were hard core cyclists. I had no money for fancy panniers, so had bought the cheapest saddle bags I could find, strapped my sleeping bag and foam mat onto my rack with a bungee cord and was good to go. To keep weight down, our teacher instructed us to pack light, so bring only two pairs of underpants, one to wear and the other to wash in the morning and then dangle from our saddlebags to dry in the wind as we rode. I think most of us opted to go commando rather than risk the embarrassment of this laundry option. We followed the California Bicentennial Bike Route, cycling along Highway One through Carmel, Santa Barbara, and along the shore of all the coastal beach towns in metro Los Angeles, camping along the way, fueled by flour tortillas and refried beans. The three-week tour cost $120, money I raised by combining Christmas money, baby-sitting savings and bike club fund raising.

Two months before the bike trip, the girl I had loved more than anyone on earth had been murdered. In the years we had been best friends, she was sunlight to me, yet I had spent the last year of her life being an idiot—jealous and stupid and mean. There's no room for do-overs with death. I was fifteen, miserable and broke, with no clue how to grieve the death of my friend. I couldn't articulate this at the time, but the trip allowed me to escape from the sorrow and loneliness that shrouded my life. It helped me begin to heal. All of this hinged on me having a bike. That ill-gotten fire-engine-red ten speed set me free.

Then it was stolen from my house. Without my dad around, our flat had become a flop house for every form of renegade teen. People flowed in and out, night and day. The front door was left unlocked and someone with bolt-cutters clipped the chain I had wrapped around the stair bannister to secure my bike. My friend had always believed in Karma, but after her murder, I hadn't given it much credence. I couldn't find a way to see Karma's place in her death, so had rejected it. Still, I was complicit in cheating a vet out of a thousand bucks by out-coloring the other poster contestants. And now my bike was gone. It felt like Karma kicking back.

I resumed walking to school, until one day a girl rode up on my bike. She was new at school, had lived in India in an Ashram or something, and had long blond hair. Her voice always sounded like a sigh.

"Hey, that's my bike," I said, when she coasted up to the front steps of our hippie school and smiled at me.

"I just bought it from Missing Link," she said, still straddling the bike, her paisley skirt pulled up between her legs and tucked into the waist. She smiled some more. Part of me didn't really want to take it back, since she was super cool and pretty and had a nose ring. But the rest of me was sick of being bikeless.

"That's totally my bike," I said. I squatted down beside the bike and ran my hand under the bottom bracket. The serial numbers were beaten off the frame, but it was definitely my bike. I had spent hours cleaning it, repacking the hubs, greasing the chain, and taping the handlebars. I knew every scratch on it.

She hiked her leg over the crossbar and leaned the bike toward me.

"Here you go," she said. Another smile. She believed in Karma too. Karma always seems to favor giving things away.

I took the bicycle, glaring at her to mask my complete joy, like wanting it too much might jinx it. Like Karma would sense my longing for material things and send another Berkeley bike thief to steal my ten-speed away again. Karma cut me some slack after that and I didn't lose another bicycle until years later when my Bianchi mountain bike disappeared. It was the most expensive bike I'd ever purchased, bought with money I inherited when my grandma died. Losing my Bianchi probably wasn't Karma at play as much as my own forgetfulness. Despite my love for that bike, when I was going up for tenure, I got so stressed out I forgot a lot of things. How to be calm. How to breathe. Where I parked my bike. I'm not 100% sure, but I think I rode my Bianchi to campus, later forgotten I had ridden it and so walked home after work. Three days later, I remembered the bike, but by then it was long gone.

I imagine Karma might have charged the thief a bit for taking that Bianchi from me, but maybe not. The bike was, after all, just a thing. This was 2002 and things like bicycles still felt affordable. I'm with Susan B. Anthony in the belief that the bicycle "has done more to emancipate women than anything else in the world." I lament the shift towards cycling as an elite and costly sport, since, as Susan B. said, the bike "gives women a feeling of freedom and self-reliance." Freedom and self-reliance, that's what I felt when I careened down the Berkeley streets as a kid and two things I've needed throughout my life. I needed freedom and self-reliance as a teen living on my own after my sister moved away. As a young woman studying math in roomfuls of men at Cal. When I left my high school teaching job to go to graduate school. When I moved to a conservative state, miles from the ocean, to start a career in academia. I wouldn't have had the courage to go where my life has gone, were it not for the bikes in my life. They set me free without costing more than I could afford. This is how I think the world should work.

US, THEM, AND THE IMPOSTER WITHIN

Cat Caperello

I bought my first bike as an adult from a department store in 2008. It was an undersized mountain bike; a little candy apple red Schwinn with a front suspension fork. It was comically too small, but I didn't know that yet because I didn't know the first thing about bikes other than that I wanted to ride one. I named it Dexter.

I bought Dexter under the pretense of commuting a few dozen blocks uptown to college. I wanted to be more active, save gas money, and avoid the stress of driving and parking in my densely packed yet strangely un-walkable neighborhood in Albany, New York. I still used my car for my work commute outside of town. I was not consciously aware of the truth, but in my heart I knew I needed this active transportation to help me save my life.

I had always been overweight. The roundness of childhood expanded with my age and enclosed me within it. I'm not sure exactly where my weight peaked in my early twenties, but I topped out somewhere around 315 or 320. The scale would show *E* for *error* and after a while, I just stopped looking. I'm sure I was pre-diabetic although health care folks prepared to cluck their tongues were always pleasantly surprised at my spot-on blood pressure. My knees, however, suffered the wrath of extra weight the most, and taking off pounds was becoming crucial if I had any hope to maintain mobility. I slowly chipped away at the weight by reframing and adjusting my food intake (*sincere thanks, Weight Watchers*) but I hit a plateau at 265 pounds. I knew it was time to add physical activity.

I was parked on my couch when bicycling called to me from a television program showing off thin people cycle touring Tuscany. Gliding there on the rolling Italian landscape, they seemed so adventurous, so free. Plus bicycles were billed as better for the knees.

Despite already losing forty pounds or so from my peak weight, I still couldn't bring myself to go to the local bike shop. I was afraid of that moment where the person at the shop is visibly uncomfortable by the idea of my weight on their merchandise; afraid of the moment they'd tell me there was nothing for me in their store because I was too heavy. How could those thin wheels hope to hold me?

And then there was the price tag associated with any brand worth carrying.

Instead I went to Target, and found my knobby-tired first love, Dexter.

I had no idea how to shop for a bike. No concept of size, nothing. I tested the bike gently by easing myself onto it and feeing how the shocks responded. I remember trying to ride down the aisles of the store, and while I was doing everything wrong, the sturdiness of that little red Schwinn with its wide tires was a big piece of the puzzle for building my confidence, both on the bike and within my body. I'll never forget the way it felt the first time I zipped around the parking lot outside, or crested a hill in Washington Square Park.

I knew immediately when I went to lock it up on a bike rack that Dexter wasn't cool—well, for a nine year old maybe, but for an overweight 29-year old white woman, not so much. It looked juvenile and out of place. I started observing other riders I would see around and noticed their bikes and how their bodies seemed to fit with the machine. I felt like a circus bear by contrast; hulking torso hunched over a too-short top tube, knees rising up so far they betrayed any "fake it till you make it" bravado.

The word 'hipster' hadn't quite come into fashion yet, but that's the group who was visibly using bikes in my neighborhood and even at college. I was not one of them, and I certainly wasn't a lycra-clad fitness cyclist either. I felt like an imposter, trying to break into this thing that only other people could have; only for the super fit or fashionable. That was who I *noticed* was riding anyway.

Perception is everything, and the lens we view the world through is tinted with our own experience.

It was when I moved to Portland, and was exposed to a diverse community that uses bicycles for all kinds of transportation that I became aware of my own myopia. I noticed so many different kinds of people riding all different kinds of bikes. Specifically, the weathered faces who brought their homes everywhere with them, and I don't mean the Tuscan cycle tourists from the television who had inspired me years ago.

Riding for transportation in Portland got me thinking: What makes a cyclist anyway? Who gets to claim this identity? Looking back, I wonder how many more people I *didn't see* at that time because of my unconscious classism regarding bikes and cycling. I had been unaware of the depths to which I was indoctrinated with my own privilege.

Truth is, I was so broke I could only afford a bicycle because Target gave me $200 worth of credit. Incidentally this was the first account in the long, slow recovery of my credit after the financial debacle known as my early 20's. In that way the bike was foundational in the restoration of my credit as well as my health. But regardless of the challenges of putting fuel in the car, my heft, or my own bike dorkiness, I still benefitted from all kinds of privilege. That's intersectionality, and knowing is half the battle.

Ask yourself honestly: does your perception of a rider change if you think they're towing a trailer with a child in it, only to learn instead it 's filled with empty cans? What if they're disheveled? Or maybe appear to be an immigrant? Or just don't *look* like you? There are a thousand ways to carve the world into us and them. Noticing these unconscious prejudices is the first step in dismantling them.

. . .

It's been nearly a decade since I first saddled up in the sporting goods section of the Target in East Greenbush, New York and everything is different in a thousand ways I could have never expected.

Dexter has long since been donated and I'm sure making some ten year old very happy—that's the age human it was made for, after all. I didn't bring my car when my partner and I moved from the East Coast to Oregon. My transportation investment went instead into a bike that I hope to enjoy for years. My current ride is a gorgeous cross bike with drop handlebars, and thin wheels. Slick black and sexy. An instant classic I call Pele and take bike camping a few times a year. It would have cost nearly 10x what the Schwinn cost if I paid retail, but thankfully I got a fantastic deal. I've put about four thousand miles on it so far.

I've been stable at 185 pounds for more than year, and although sometimes the 120ish pounds I've lost—or my transplant status in a radically gentrifying city—still hang on me like an unshakable dysmorphia, I am so thankful to feel more at home than ever in my body, on the bike, and in the world.

PUT THE FUN BETWEEN YOUR LEGS

Joe Biel

In 1995 my Ford was totaled in a terrible crash when another car ran a red light. A few months later another car I was driving was accordianed by a snowplow. Simultaneously realizing the real risk to my life and the absurd economics behind my choice to drive, I became a bicycle commuter. Such things were not yet in fashion as a cost-savings for the city, let alone as a healthy choice for the individual—especially not on the eastside of Cleveland, where I lived.

My upbringing had been brutal. Beatings were routine in my household. My dad was disabled after a stroke and couldn't walk or talk clearly. I lived with undiagnosed Autism. My family lived on money from social security and disability. Threats and screaming were constant. I lived in fear. It was miserable to be at home so about the time I turned twelve I would ride my bike to the comic shop or record store to escape. When I was old enough to move out, I did, and continued my trips by bike. But it didn't always make me popular. Once, some punks egged me as I rode by and another time they tried to throw my bike down a sewer.

In 1996, as an eighteen-year-old, I founded Microcosm Publishing, a bicycle propaganda emporium and book publisher. I began scheming up slogans for stickers and t-shirts on long interstate bike rides and one of my crown jewels was "Put the Fun Between Your Legs," with the words surrounding a picture of a bicycle. It was an instant hit, though admittedly I hadn't realized the implied sexual nature of *why* some people thought it was so brilliant. Nonetheless, I began printing the shirts in my basement—now in Portland, OR—as the orders came in.

As time went by it began to make more sense to order 50 shirts from a print shop and then 100 and then hundreds. By 2005, when bicycle commuting had really become hip, I had sold over 5,000 of them. The next year, bicycling exploded in Portland, OR and the shirt became an even bigger hit. Bootlegs started to appear, which were flattering until major companies began to bootleg the design as well. Google became flooded with hundreds of exact copies and it was becoming increasingly difficult for people who wanted to buy the t-shirt to find my legitimate version. By 2015, after sending hundreds of pleading requests for people all over the world to stop stealing my work, I buckled and registered the trademark. Three months later I found out that someone we will call "Mr. Pink" had registered a

similar mark days before mine with one word changed and an identical image composition.

I spent hours on the phone with the trademark office in Washington, DC. How could Mr. Pink trademark something that is so clearly based on my work? Apparently he could by claiming to be unaware of my image—which had now sold over 25,000 prints and had reached all corners of the bicycle community. At the urging of the trademark attorney, I found a lawyer to review my case. He explained how expensive a lawsuit or opposing this other person's mark would be. I decided to simply get in touch with the claimant and explain that licensing my original image would be cheaper than filing a trademark and having me contest it. I wrote a friendly and pleasant email titled "Working Together." For two months there was no response. I started to worry. I could see that he had hired a lawyer to file his claim, though I learned from talking to the trademark office that many parts of it were out of order.

I looked up Mr. Pink's website and found that he was using my design to raise money for "at risk youth" to get into the outdoors. Starting to get a little panicked, I sent him a letter and another email, explaining my situation politely. I didn't care if he continued to use the image, but because he had filed his trademark a few weeks before mine, his claim had the potential to hold mine in limbo.

Finally, Mr. Pink responded to my email with bullet points that had been copied and pasted from another email, presumably from his lawyer. He claimed to not care about trademarking the image, that its similarity to my own design was a complete coincidence, and that he was not going to pay me or rescind his application. He signed the message "Peacolaaaaa!"

The message felt jarring, authoritative, and final. Trademark law was new to me. I had tried to eke out a safe place in the universe to write bicycle slogans and this phenomenon that I had created had gone viral and had been an important part of my ability to earn income for a particularly difficult period of my life. The bootlegging had impaired my ability to support myself. Dave Griffiths, a local, disabled, homeless activist explained to me that "Privilege is when you assume that power structures will do things for you. A lack of privilege is when you fear that power structures will do things that harm you." The system works for people like Mr. Pink. Coming from a place of entitlement with his emails coached by his lawyer, he approaches the world from a position of privilege. And then it occurred to me: I was exactly the kind of person that Mr. Pink was intending to raise money for; a former "at-risk youth" who wouldn't have gotten out of the house if it wasn't for my bicycle. But through the distance of the Internet I must have seemed like a meddling adult from a far away world with even greater resources than he has.

Mr. Pink is in his 20s and is starting a white savior organization. He lives with his parents in a far-flung exurb that is 94% white and above the median income line with a poverty rate one quarter of the national average. There's an adage in bicycle advocacy that people who grew up in relative privilege discover bicycling in traffic and for the first time in their lives find out what it feels like to be disempowered, threatened, and be wrongly judged. I had known plenty of people who had turned to bicycle advocacy without connecting it to the struggles that other people experience every day. It's a bit of a tired narrative for me, honestly.

I can't resent Mr. Pink for the privilege he was born into but I can resent how he uses it. I spent the following year nervously checking in on his filing once per week. Neither Mr. Pink nor his lawyer had responded to the Trademark Office's request for more information about his inaccurate filing and his application was rejected. My application was reviewed and finally in 2016 it was approved. When I got in touch with Mr. Pink again a year later to inform him that I was writing this story, his lawyer informed me that he had abandoned the organization and stopped using the image. Also, the lawyer said, Mr. Pink would prosecute me for writing a story identifying him.

Perhaps the difference between him and I is that I find meaning and purpose by connecting my own experience to the struggles of others through empathy. I had to fight for everything that I have built. And my reasons for printing and distributing messages of empowerment haven't changed one iota in 22 years.

ODE TO THE FIXIE!!!

Kassandra Karaitis

I live in Southern California. People don't ride bikes here. Well, they do, but the status of a fancy car is too important to have a lot of cyclists.

I grew up in Chicago. Bike messengers were my heroes, so, when I lived there, I commuted by bicycle in the weather, year round. They did! Why couldn't I? Sure, riding in negative temperatures was hard! The wind was rough! But it felt cheaper to ride than take public transportation. It also felt faster than public transportation; I could ride door to door—anywhere I wanted to go; I didn't have to wait for buses or trains to show up and, well—I love the solitary quality of riding a bike. But, the weather in Chicago took its toll on me. When I graduated from grad school, I moved to Southern California, to find a Real Job.

The first year I lived here, I was miserable. What the hell did I do? I didn't like Chicago, but, other than the stellar weather, Southern California almost felt worse. I rarely rode. I saw my bike every day, hanging on the ceiling like a sad sculpture, and it made me cry. Finally, one day, I started to ride again. Every day. It made me happy...and I decided to look for another job where more cycling would be possible. After some time, I found a job in which I could finally, proudly say I had a "career." More importantly, though, they had showers in the break room...and I could ride my bike to work!

Almost a year went past and I woke up in a hospital bed. The first thing I did was head straight to the window and look for my bike. The doctors and nurses were so excited and I had no idea why. Apparently, while riding my bike home from work, I was hit by an SUV. I was unconscious when I was brought in, and I had been in a medically induced coma for thirteen days. I had suffered a severe brain trauma and a concussion. My C1 vertebrae was fractured—and according to my neurosurgeons, it was "a miracle I could walk!" They attributed that to my wearing a helmet. Luckily, I had insurance.

Some say I am oddly proud for giving up my career due to a cycling accident, but realizing that I was riding my bike home from countless soul-sucking jobs meant my life would never be the same. Life is too short to waste my time doing something I hated for at least ten hours every day. What saved me was the bike ride to work...but, the irony that almost getting killed coming home from a place I couldn't stand was too much. I have severe PTSD, so, I quit my job and am now on disability. But you can't keep me off my bike. Besides my cat, that's what I live for (and he's no good on a bike—his feet don't reach the pedals). Riding keeps me sane. I have rearranged my entire schedule so I can ride when there are less cars. I wake up at 3am every morning to meditate and at 4:30am I am out the door, ready to ride for as long as I want. Barely anyone is on the road, so, my PTSD has extremely lessened.

I can honestly say that a day I don't take even a short ride is a day I feel depressed, tired, and don't want to do much.

I have spent less money on my bicycles and their maintenance than the cumulative sum I have spent on therapists in my lifetime...and riding a bike helps me more than talking to any therapist ever has.

To me, my bicycles are not cheap. Maybe I'm really attached to them. Maybe I'm not particularly good at sharing, but they feel like a huge part of me and I miss them if one of them has to be in the shop for any length of time. I don't lock them up, outside—I walk when I do errands. I keep them inside at night. This way, anyone with sticky fingers has less chance of riding off with them. Someone else might get $25-$100 for them? I have no idea. My bikes give me a freedom cars don't. They bring me happiness driving in a car never has. How does one put a price tag on that?

Since my accident, my attitude towards money has changed significantly. I know it's a good month when I can get my cat his food, treats, and anything else he might need and get a tune-up for a bike, if it needs it, pay my bills...and eat well. The mere fact that I can do these things and be happy without worrying about other, meaningless things feels pretty damned good.

I might be what most consider "poor", but, with my bicycles, I feel way richer than I ever felt with any job I've ever had and, frankly, I finally feel like I just don't care what others think...as long as they know I'm there when I'm riding past them!

THE UNTOKENING: A REFLECTION AND NEXT STEPS

Norma Herrera-Bacon

"Equity" is quite the buzzword amongst mobility justice organizations. I would know, I used to work for one. The organization I worked for, the California Bicycle Coalition, or CalBike for short, uses that word a lot. The idea is that by advocating for infrastructure in communities that are often ignored by government agencies, they'll be somehow fixing a wealth of issues related to transportation. And while they genuinely want to fight and work for the underserved people and communities in our beautiful state, they—like many other similar organizations—fall a bit short of succeeding. The issue, I think, is a lack of inclusivity.

Who are "underserved people?" The term is broad but they tend to be poor, and people of color. In other words, people like me. Add in the fact that I'm a woman and the child of immigrants and you've got the perfect token for your organization.

So when I read Sahra Sulaiman's essay on Streetsblog LA about a new transportation conference called The Untokening— which she opens with a story from the 2015 CalBike Summit—I felt the overwhelming need to attend. The Untokening took place in Atlanta on November 13th, 2016 and was put on by a committee of women and people of color. It was put together with the understanding that if we are ever to fix transportation issues, we must also face the other issues affecting our communities: gentrification, police brutality, harassment in all its forms, violence. I applied for a scholarship and let my colleagues know that I would be going whether I got it or not (I did).

The Untokening was a first and foremost a healing experience, especially after the trauma from Election Day only a few days before. Being in a space dominated by women and people of color from all over the country was a powerful experience that continues to inspire me daily more than six months later and will likely inspire me for the rest of my life. We were able to talk freely about the issues we face as advocates for better mobility. Issues of feeling unworthy because of our skin color, our gender, our lack of a degree. Feeling pushed out of the very communities we work in because of gentrification and a nationwide housing crisis. Feeling like we're crazy because the people we're often in meetings with don't understand where we're coming from, why we're talking about social justice when we should - or so they feel—be talking about bikes. Simply, they don't understand our experiences.

The plan is to have many more Untokenings throughout the country. You can find out when at their website (www.untokening.org). Until then, I present some tips, which I've compiled based on experience and discussions had in Atlanta, on *how to become a better ally in the bike advocacy world:*

- Do not expect community leaders (the people leading bike rides, who are part of the culture; the ones you call disenfranchised) to speak eloquently—code for "talk white"; understand that we are not all as educated as you, that this is the way we talk in our communities. Speaking in Spanglish or Ebonics, with accents and simple words is how we're *understood in our communities.*

- Respect our experience and accept that we have a lot to learn from each other. You can take all the urban planning classes you want, but if you don't know how our communities actually work, your bike lanes and road diets will fail.

- Accept that the bicycle, as in the actual transportation tool, does not belong only to white/young/male/middle-class/athletic/typically-abled/fast   people. Recognize that your advocacy should be for the masses, and if you want your work to succeed, you need to check yourself when working with those masses.

- Do not be condescending to the people you see as an embarrassment. Not everyone can afford a nice bicycle. Not everyone wants the newest model. Some of us love our sticker-covered beaters.

- Smile to the migrant workers riding their mountain bikes, offer them an extra light if you can, carry around information about bike safety in different languages.

- The person who rides 5 miles a day deserves as much respect as the person who rides 50.

- We do not need to regularly do centuries to know our stuff. Not all of us are physically capable of mashing up hills all the time. I am not, and will never be, impressed by your mileage - it does not make you a better advocate than me.

- It is ableist, ageist and elitist to disparage ebikes. Some people need the assist to be able to ride a bike; do you really prefer they drive?

- Take your outreach to the people. The expectation that people of lower-incomes can take time off work to come to your meetings is unrealistic and unfair. Look at the success of programs like LACBC's Operation Firefly, which gives free lights to passing bicyclists in Los Angeles; they're actually out in the underserved communities providing a tangible benefit.

- Look beyond academics to the people in the community already doing the work. Experience matters as much if not more than formal education. People without degrees tend to value experience more.

- Engage organizations that already exist.

- Do not present problems that you think exist, ask community members what they want.

- Diversity in the bike advocacy world already exists. You just have to look.

- Listen. Listen. Listen.

- Bikes lanes are not enough. We need to face issues of police brutality, housing, and income inequality. A majority of folks at The Untokening felt that solutions that are only infrastructure based are not enough. We can, and we should, use our work to draw attention to larger social issues. Intersectionality is important, and is ultimately how our movement will survive.

Beyond the bike lane, the bicycle can be a tool for social change. I look forward to continuing the fight on two wheels and taking back our streets for a safer and more inclusive future.

Join me.

Fiction

THE CUSS WORD

Lauren Hage

"I dare ya!" screamed Bryan, the portly boy that lived across the way from me, as we rode feverishly on our bikes toward the railway overpass to see what his older brother had graffitied.

"Ahhh!... Okay. FUUUCK!" I yelled at the top of my lungs, followed by a girlish giggle. That was the first time I had ever said a cuss word out loud in public. Bryan followed by yelling every four letter word he could think of, including "BOOB!"

We braked hard on the powdery gravel underneath the train bridge, creating a cloud of dust around our feet, momentarily hiding the numerous cigarette butts, broken beer bottles, cold medicine blister packs, and the occasional syringe.

"See, this is what my brother did! Ain't it awesome?" said Bryan, snorting and wiping his nose on his sleeve.

"Cool!" I said, nodding my head. I was around nine years old. This was the first time I had ever seen graffiti up close and personal. Before, I had only seen it on the trains whizzing by our car, when waiting for one to pass; they were just blurs of colors. While taking it all in, I heard a car off in the distance.

"Oh-shit-the-cops!" Bryan said, in one long strung-together word. We hopped on our bikes and headed toward the alleyway between our houses. Luckily, the plume of gravel dust made a temporary curtain between us and the patrol car coming up the road.

"Here! Let's ditch our bikes and hide in the bushes!" I panted. Bryan nodded and we quickly jumped off our bikes. As they spun wobbling down the alley toward their sure fall on the side of the embankment, we hid in Mrs. Gavinson's garden—between the bushes lining the alley and a row of tomato plants.

We sat quietly. Sweat dripped from Bryan's forehead into his eyes, making him blink over and over. My heart was pounding. The patrol officer had stopped at the end of the road, deciding which way to go and taking a sip of his coffee. That's when it hit me...

"I have an idea," I muttered, with a sneaky smile. I picked out one of the rotten tomatoes that Mrs. Gavinson had neglected to pick. It was probably too hard for her to bend down so far to get it, being the oldest lady on the block. Bryan snickered at the idea and found a tomato of his own. Just as the cop car lurched forward, I whispered, "Now!"

We launched our tomatoes and watched as one smashed a gooey red mess over the front of the windshield and the other landed on the top, making the loudest thump I could imagine. We giggled at the scene as the cop stopped abruptly and turned on his wipers. He got out of his car and looked around. Befuddled, he got back in and changed trajectories. He swerved over and started down the alley.

"Oh man!" Bryan said, almost forgetting that we needed to be quiet.

"It's cool, just keep calm. He can't see us here," I murmured, trying to keep the tomato flies from getting into my mouth. The policeman drove even slower now, the crunching of the gravel getting louder and louder. Just then, Mrs. Gavinson opened her back door holding a bag of trash.

"Just be very quiet. She can't see very well without her glasses on," I said, and Bryan agreed. We turned our attention back toward the cop. He was now so close to us we could feel the hot and smelly exhaust blowing through the bushes, onto our faces. We tried not to cough. Then with the sound of Mrs. Gavinson closing the lid on her old rusty trash can, the police car stopped. He'd had his windows down to hear any goings on. Through a break in the leaves I could see his face as he looked over toward the old lady. Then, giving up on his mysterious tomato case, he turned his radio back on, rolled up his windows, and drove away. Once we couldn't hear his tires anymore, we stood up and brushed the dirt off our knees.

"Wow that was a close one," Bryan chuckled, "I should get home, it's close to suppertime. If I'm late again I'll get a whoopin.'"

"Okay, see ya tomorrow," I said, picking up my bike and looking down at the price tag that had been hastily ripped off. This was my second bike. The first had been taken from me by my step-dad a couple years back to do some kind of welding practice, as a punishment for my attempt to run away from home, only to get pulled over by a policeman who noticed me biking down the long levy—which looks strange when you are only seven years old. I wondered if it had been the same cop?

      I opened the back door of my house—leaving my bike in the tall grass, waiting for my next adventure.

Recipe

A FOODIE'S CONFESSION: A RECIPE FOR A BICYCLE

Adrian Lipscombe

I have two loves in life, food and bicycling. I never knew how much food and bicycling went together till I got a bike and I always found myself hungry when I rode my bike. Well, yeah, the more I ride, the hungrier I am. I would always find myself navigating to the closest foodie spots. As I would ride by those food trailers and restaurants I could smell the deliciousness they have to offer and demand a U-turn to investigate. Bikes have allowed me to slow down and find those hole-in-the-wall places that serve something you cannot find going 50 mph. When burning those calories, I get the urge to roll into the closest taco joint or hole-in-wall that is sporting more bike parking than car parking. Those are my favorite places to go.

Food and bikes have so much in common. With food it has always been about the quality of the food and the flavor, and as a bicyclist it has been about the bike and the ride. They each cannot live without the other. Commonly, they are both social activities. They both bring people together for good reasons and leave people in a euphoria of happiness.

To spread the love of food and bicycling. I suggest making some Get Around Town Brownies. This is my go-to recipe for something sweet and it is awesome to share with friends.

Get Around Town Brownie

1 ½ cups flour

½ teaspoon baking soda

½ teaspoon salt

⅔ cups butter

1 ½ cups sugar

4 tablespoons water

24 ounces semi sweet chocolate chips, divided

2 teaspoons vanilla

4 eggs

1 cup of nuts (optional)

Preheat oven to 325 degrees. In a small bowl, combine flour, baking soda, and salt; set aside. In a small saucepan, combine butter, sugar, and water. Bring just to a boil, and then remove from heat. Add half of the chocolate chips and all the vanilla extract. Stir until chocolate chips melt and mixture is smooth. Transfer the chocolate mixture to a large bowl. Add eggs, one at a time, beating well after each addition. Gradually blend in flour mixture. Stir in remaining chocolate chips and the nuts. Place in two 9 x 14 inch pans. Bake for 20-22 minutes.

ABOUT THE CONTRIBUTORS

Dr. Adonia E. Lugo is an anthropologist who focuses on social movements and sustainable transportation. She teaches, writes, and speaks about her ongoing exploration of urban space, race, and mobility. Her essay here is adapted from her book *Bicycle/Race: Transportation, Culture, and Resistance* (Microcosm Publishing, 2018).

Adrian Lipscombe sees herself as an instigator within the community by bringing awareness and advocacy through forms of place-making, tactical urbanism, and food justice. She is currently in the process of getting her Ph.D. in the Community and Regional Planning program at the University of Texas at Austin, concentrating her studies on the attitude and behavior of minorities towards transportation and land use. She played a major role in the development with the San Antonio and Austin bike share system. With her Masters in Architecture, she is the founder and Principal of Urbanlocity Design firm. She invest her time with communities by consulting, creating and assisting on place making and tactical planning projects such as AustinSOUP, VIVA Streets ATX, Take it to the Table project, her restaurant in La Cross, Wisconsin, and her blog www. AdieEats.com.

Cat Caperello is a writer, bike nerd and open road enthusiast who loves helping indie entrepreneurs tell their story online, and encouraging more women to try on riding bikes and bike camping IRL. When she's not out riding or quieting the voices in her head with pen and paper, Cat enjoys cooking, long walks with her super mutt, Ziggy, copious amounts of coffee, and feeling good. Say howdy at girleatsbike.com, she don't bite.

Do Jun Lee is a bike scholar and activist in Environmental Psychology at the Graduate Center of the City University of New York. He writes a blog on people, mobility, place and justice at intersectionalriding.com, where his essay here was originally published.

Gretchin Lair is a benevolent bureaucrat, pretend patient, unfinished poet and obsolete geek. She is allergic to coercion, especially if it is marketed as a benefit. gretchin@scarletstarstudios.com

Joe Biel is a self-made publisher and filmmaker who draws origins, inspiration, and methods from punk rock. He is the founder/manager of Microcosm Publishing and co-founder of the Portland Zine Symposium. He tours with his films on the Dinner and Bikes program and has been featured in *Time Magazine, Publisher's Weekly, Utne Reader, Portland Mercury, Oregonian, Broken Pencil, Readymade, Punk Planet, Profane Existence, Spectator* (Japan), *G33K* (Korea), and *Maximum Rocknroll*. He is the author of many books, including *Good Trouble: Building a Successful Life & Business with Autism.* He is the director of several documentaries, most recently *Aftermass: Bicycling in a Post-Critical Mass Portland* and the Groundswell film series.

Julie Brooks is a writer, rider, bicycling activist and roving researcher of the wholly remarkable galaxy of Upstate New York. She is the co-editor of the zine *Pedal by Pedal: Women Over Forty on Bicycling and Life*, and is working on a collection of essays about bicycling and social dilemmas.

Kassandra Karaitis is an avid cyclist, surfer, meditator, yogi and a beginning parkour practitioner. If she isn't camping or hiking, she can be seen writing and curling up with her beloved cat, Hobbes, and a good book.

Katura Reynolds went car-free in 2009 and has been rising to the challenge of potlucks by bike/bus/train ever since. She lives in Seattle and tweets as @katura_art.

Lauren Hage can be found shipping your package at Microcosm, playing with her cats, or reading at the park. In between all those endeavors she is most likely creating art, which you can view a small sample of on her website:

Norma Herrera-Bacon has been an activist for safer streets since 2010 and believes bikes can make the world a better place. Check out her website at normalizebicycling.org

Phill Melton used to live, write, and ride around Washington, DC. He's since moved to Austin, Texas to find new ways to make trouble on bikes. He has somehow become "the bike nut" to his coffee and pottery friends, and "the coffee and pottery nut" to his bike friends. He has an inordinate fondness for loud socks and bike hats with kittens and butterflies.

Rebecca Fish Ewan has yet to finish her bike tour across the States (the short way) interrupted 30 years ago by a snow storm in Utah. Writer, cartoonist, author of a CNF book, *A Land Between*, Rebecca has also published in *Brevity, Hip Mama*, and *Landscape Architecture*, and just launched a walking zine called *GRAPH(feeties)*. Twitter: @rfishewan Website: rebeccafishewan. com

Rhienna Renée Guedry is a Louisiana-born weirdo who found her way to the Pacific Northwest, perhaps solely to get use out of her extensive outerwear collection. A Jill of All Trades, she balances her time as best she can between Producing at a digital agency, volunteering at the Sundance Film Festival, DJing, and curating the best Halloween parties this side of the Mason-Dixon. Rhienna also holds a MS in Writing/Publishing from Portland State University. Her writing has appeared in *Bitch Magazine*, *Taking the Lane*, *Cypress Dome*, and various other publications you've probably never heard of. Her Twitter alter egos are @djrhienna and @chouchootPDX

Sidnee Haynes. Short woman. Hard worker. Big eater.

Tamika L. Butler, Esq. is a proud Nebraskan living Los Angeles as the Executive Director of the Los Angeles County Bicycle Coalition. Previously, she was the Director of Social Change Strategies at Liberty Hill Foundation, where she oversaw the foundation's boys and men of color program and LGBTQ grant strategy. Before Liberty Hill, Tamika worked at Young Invincibles fighting for the economic rights of her fellow millennials. A Stanford Law educated lawyer, she transitioned to policy work after litigating for three years as an employment lawyer at Legal Aid Society-Employment Law Center. Her essay here is adapted from a piece originally published on Facebook.

Texas-based poet and performance artist **Tammy Melody Gomez** premiered her first theater play, *She: Bike/Spoke/ Love* in 2007 to fulfill a dream of depicting the urban bicycling culture and the poetry of cycling. Her literary work has been published widely, in collections such as *Women in Nature: An Anthology* (Louise Grace Publishing, 2014), *The Beatest State in the Union: an Anthology of Beat Texas Writing* (Lamar University Press, 2016), and *Entre Guadalupe y Malinche: Tejanas in Literature and Art* (UT Press, 2016). Tammy is a 2015-2018 Black Earth Institute Fellow and more can be learned about her here: www.hatchfund.org/user/tammygomez

V. K. Henry is a poet, writer, and rare book specialist. She is currently working on a nonfiction book on safer ways to leave abusive relationships, and two urban fantasy novels. She loves fancy leggings and unsweet iced tea.

GUAYAKÍ
·BRAND·
YERBA MATE

COME TO LIFE